What People Are Saying About

Christian Thinking through the Ages

Christian Thinking through the Ages is an outstanding and exceptional book, which brings coherence to a complex history of ideas and controversy. I wish it had been available some fifty years ago when I was studying theology at university.
HILARY ANSLOW OBE, former Principal of King George V College, Southport.

This little book is a colourful mosaic of the great Christian tradition. Its profound learning is both lively and readable. Balanced and open-minded, it will stimulate the faithful and encourage the not-so-faithful — altogether a remarkable achievement.
Dr PETER NEWMAN BROOKS, Life Fellow, Robinson College, Cambridge.

Christians reading this book may well feel that its concentration on Jesus's teaching and that of his followers results in losing sight of his "person" as the human face of God. It is, nevertheless, a lucid account of theological trends and controversies over the centuries, and it bears all the hallmarks of an experienced teacher of history.
The Rt Revd and Rt Hon LORD CHARTRES, GCVO, ChStJ, PC, FSA, FBS, former Bishop of London.

This book's chapters deftly and expertly trace the distinct epochs of Christian thought. There is an unstinting and illuminating focus on the significance of Christ as teacher and an accompanying alertness to the instructional potential of epistles, commentaries and other text types in the Christian tradition.

ROGER DALRYMPLE, Professor of Practice in Lifelong Learning and Senior Research Fellow in Education, Regent's Park College, Oxford.

I am delighted to recommend this clear and enlightened history of Christian thought. David Arnold begins with Jesus Christ, and leads us through the ages, through the twists and turns of history, to the present day, explaining with great clarity how the faith was affected by the times, and reflecting on where Christian thought is going now.

The Revd ALAN MAYER, formerly Rector of St Mary's, Oxted, Surrey, and author of *A Grand Tour of Faith, Life, and Time* and *Zen Questions for Christians*.

This is an impressive book — impressive for its great breadth of knowledge, its lucidity in handling complex issues, its ever sensible and fair-minded judgment, and its humaneness. But it is most impressive for its coherence between the author's account in the first chapter of his own developing Christianity over his life and his approach to most of the great Christian writers in history.

HENRY MAYR-HARTING, Emeritus Regius Professor of Ecclesiastical History in the University of Oxford.

This lucid history of Christianity's Big Ideas, from the Gospel of Jesus of Nazareth to the literal interpretation of the Bible by Evangelical Christians, sheds light on the great conundrums the faithful have had to contend with, over 2000 years. What is

meant by "God is Love"? Does the Divine transcend gender, or is God a woman? What was the purpose of the crucifixion? David Arnold does not presume to know all the answers, but the quest he leads us on is satisfying nonetheless.
CRISTINA ODONE, former Editor of the *Catholic Herald.*

At a time when many thoughtful people no longer believe that Christian thought could make any real difference to their life, one or two may hesitate and reflect that just possibly it may be a mistake to commit two millennia of Christian wisdom to the dustbin. Entertainingly and lucidly David Arnold will, in this compendium, take the reader through the amazing and often bewildering legacy of Jesus of Nazareth and his interpreters who, like it or not, have laid the foundations of our threatened civilization. If that feels too daunting, just to read the author's personal prologue will, I predict, make you dive in.
The Revd Canon Dr PAUL OESTREICHER OBE, former Director of the International Centre for Reconciliation at Coventry Cathedral.

David Arnold has a wonderful capacity for undertaking extensive research into historical and theological literature and representing it in a manner accessible to all. His style is easy and straightforward, making acquiring knowledge an exciting adventure.
The Revd Canon DEREK TANSILL, former Vicar of Horsham and Chaplain to Chichester Cathedral.

The real excitement of reading *Christian Thinking through the Ages* comes from discovering that it is not what you expected. It is neither a complete history nor an apology for the Christian faith. It is neither purely intellectual nor cloyingly evangelical.

Written by an academic, teaching historian, it is a helpful compilation of the main thrusts of Christian theological exploration down 2000 years and more. It comes to grips with the threads of thought which keep reappearing in different colours to produce a whole, but unfinished, tapestry.

David Arnold has done this in a very accessible way and the book will be invaluable to would be theologians as well as to many others who simply want to go beyond simplistic answers to the questions which Christianity poses.

However, to call the book merely a helpful compendium of thought would not do it full justice. Arnold writes in such an easy and personal way that the reader becomes aware of being invited on to a pilgrimage, where the journey is more important than the destination. By the end of the book, this reader felt he was part of the story and was being encouraged to go on exploring.

The Rt Revd MICHAEL TURNBULL CBE, former Bishop of Durham.

Christian Thinking through the Ages

Christian Thinking through the Ages

David Arnold

CHRISTIAN ALTERNATIVE
BOOKS

London, UK
Washington, DC, USA

CollectiveInk

First published by Christian Alternative Books, 2024
Christian Alternative Books is an imprint of Collective Ink Ltd.,
Unit 11, Shepperton House, 89 Shepperton Road, London, N1 3DF
office@collectiveinkbooks.com
www.collectiveinkbooks.com
www.christian-alternative.com

For distributor details and how to order please visit the 'Ordering' section on our website.

Text copyright: David Arnold 2023

ISBN: 978 1 80341 615 1
978 1 80341 635 9 (ebook)
Library of Congress Control Number: 2023943239

A CIP catalogue record for this book is available from the British Library.

Design: Lapiz Digital Services

UK: Printed and bound by CPI Group (UK) Ltd, Croydon, CR0 4YY
Printed in North America by CPI GPS partners

We operate a distinctive and ethical publishing philosophy in
all areas of our business, from our global network of authors to
production and worldwide distribution.

Other Books by This Author

Contents

To the many Christians who regularly attend church or chapel but are unsure about what they really believe, to those who think of themselves as agnostic Christians, those who think of themselves as Christians in exile, and those of any faith or none who have realized that it is better to go on seeking truth rather than imagining that they have found it.

.

Acknowledgements

It would be impossible to acknowledge all the books and all the conversations which, over a long life, have contributed to this book. They helped to form my life and they helped to form this book. I have also on Sundays, for more than seventy years, listened in Anglican parish churches or in school and college chapels to lessons read from the Bible and to sermons. Sometimes what is read or said is illuminating, but quite often it is not, and there is very little teaching in sermons about how the Christian faith has developed over the centuries.

In retirement, and in a limited way, I made an attempt to fill that gap for the ordinary parishioner where I lived with two series of lectures. The first was about how the institution known as the church developed; the second was about the development of the faith which that church proclaims. I am grateful to all those who came to the lectures and challenged my ideas. The second of those series of lectures developed into this book.

Most of all I am grateful to my wife, Cathy, and my sons, James and Piers, each of whom read the first draft and offered both encouragement and constructive criticism. One outcome of that was that I completely re-wrote two chapters. They particularly wanted me to express more clearly for a twenty-first-century audience ideas which were important in past centuries but now often seem either irrelevant to any understanding of the faith or unintelligible. I hope they have succeeded.

A Personal Prologue

Anyone writing about history should aim to avoid bias and shine light on past events rather than generate heat. But light generates at least some heat, and it is difficult to offer a historical explanation without at least implying some commendation or condemnation. So one needs to recognise, or at least attempt to recognise, one's own bias.

I write as an elderly Englishman, born in 1933, almost fifteen years after the armistice of 11 November in 1918, which postponed for just over twenty years, at least in Europe, the great world conflict which was resumed in the 1930s, reached a climax of horror in 1945, and in some ways is still continuing today, twenty-three years into the third millennium since the birth of Jesus of Nazareth.

I was five when the second phase of the European fighting began in 1939, and was evacuated from the London suburb where I lived to the Essex coast. Nine months later, after the evacuation from Dunkirk of a defeated British army, my twin brother and I returned home to Woodford Bridge in what is now the London Borough of Redbridge in time for the Battle of Britain and then the Blitz of 1940–41, spending each night in an Anderson shelter in the garden. At the age of ten I experienced the V1s and the V2s, the *Vergeltungswaffen*, or "revenge weapons", which were Germany's last desperate bid for victory in the autumn of 1944. I grew up with a strong bias against Germany and German ideas.

That autumn I went away to school at Christ's Hospital, where I encountered the teaching of Jesus of Nazareth. Every day of the week we marched to chapel. I heard the scriptures read both then and at house prayers in the evenings, and was struck by the contrast between his teaching and the world around me, both the behaviour of those immediately around me and all that was happening in the world. I gradually decided that I was a Christian (there was no sudden conversion), and at the age of fourteen, together with my twin brother (we were not identical but were very close in our thinking and attitudes) was baptised on a Friday, confirmed the following day, and went to communion for the first time on the next.

Of all the sermons I heard on Sundays throughout the eight years I was at Christ's Hospital one of the few I remembered was by a Franciscan friar who suggested remembering the acronym ACTS when praying, with those letters standing for Adoration, Confession, Thanksgiving and Supplication. I conscientiously followed his advice for many years, but I was never very good at praying. The first three I could manage, but in a world in which millions of British, German, Russian, American and Italian parents and wives prayed to the Christian God for the lives of their sons and husbands, while millions were killed, I could not see that their prayers were being answered. It was a problem which exercised me for years.

We sang at least one hymn in chapel every day, and each Saturday morning the whole school practised the hymns for the following week. One which fascinated but puzzled me was *In no strange land* by Francis Thompson:

O world invisible we view thee,
O world intangible we touch thee,
O world unknowable we know thee,
Inapprehensible, we clutch thee.

Does the fish soar to find the ocean,
The eagle plunge to find the air –
That we ask of the stars in motion
If they have rumour of thee there?

Not where the wheeling systems darken,
And our benumbed conceiving soars! –
The drift of pinions, would we hearken,
Beats at our own clay-shuttered doors.

The angels keep their ancient places:
Turn but a stone and start a wing!
'Tis ye, 'tis your estrangéd faces, –
That miss the many-splendored thing.

But (when so sad thou canst not sadder)
Cry; – and upon thy so sore loss
Shall shine the traffic of Jacob's ladder
Pitched between Heaven and Charing Cross.

Yea, in the night, my soul, my daughter
Cry, – clinging Heaven by the hems;
And lo, Christ walking on the water,
Not of Gennesareth, but Thames!

I suppose we sang it about once a term throughout the time I was at Christ's Hospital, from the age of ten to the age of eighteen, and by the time I left it had influenced my attitude to Christianity more than any other hymn.

Only a few months after leaving school, when doing my National Service, I found myself serving in a Polish unit of the British Army of the Rhine, then still an occupying army and controlling the British zone in the north of Germany. The Poles were serving with us because their country had been destroyed in September 1939 when Nazi Germany and the USSR, the Union of Soviet Socialist Republics, were allies. At the end of the war in 1945 Poland, instead of being liberated, was occupied by one of its enemies, the USSR, which was now among the victorious allies.

Already at that stage in my life, having learnt German at school, and before going up to university, I was aware that there was a sense in which the centre of European civilization, which had moved north from Italy to France in the eighteenth century, had in the nineteenth century moved to Germany. Germans were in the forefront of music and literature, the study of history, of philosophy, of theology and the new techniques of biblical criticism. At the same time they were among the leaders of the world in mathematics, science and engineering. By the end of the nineteenth century most of the multifarious German states had come together in a German Empire. It was an impressive union. They developed a system of social care before any other country, a powerful army and an increasingly powerful navy.

But the German Empire had been forged in battle, and it was the zeal of Germany's military leadership for another war to ensure Germany's predominance in Europe which, more than anything else, plunged Europe into the fighting of 1914. After losing that conflict in 1918 and suffering in the 1920s, the Germans had in the 1930s accepted, and in many cases enthusiastically followed, a government which eventually enslaved many of the citizens of neighbouring countries in the service of the German war machine.

The full extent of its extermination policies was not known until the end of the war, but what was known to anyone who did not hide from the truth was that political opponents of Nazism somehow disappeared, together with all people of Jewish origin, including those of Jewish or partly Jewish origin who were Christians and agnostics, as well people who were disabled and seen by the Nazis as no use to society, and also any others whom the Nazis regarded as undesirable, such as gypsies and homosexuals.

It was not until I went to university in 1954 that I became aware of Christians of other traditions than the Church of England. The Poles I had served with were Roman Catholics, but we had never discussed religion. Now I met both Roman Catholics and Protestant evangelicals. I found that I could talk with Roman Catholics and find where we agreed and where we differed. I found it more difficult to talk with evangelicals, who often adopted a literal interpretation of the Bible, without always having understood what they had read, and were inclined to avoid discussion with anyone who had not experienced a Pauline conversion and was not clearly of their own persuasion.

I saw my own position as being traditional, middle-of-the-road Anglicanism. I was interested in the sort of theological issues that had engaged the church for centuries and saw them as a helpful base from which to follow the Way and seek the Truth and the Life represented by Jesus. I valued the guidance of the church on both faith and morals, and at the same time valued even more the fact that it was possible to disagree. I valued the Old Testament as a collection of Hebrew writings which give an account of how ideas about God developed, and the New Testament for what it tells us about Jesus of Nazareth and about the ideas and way of looking at things which he taught.

While reading history at Oxford I was influenced by Herbert Butterfield's book *Christianity and History*, which had been published as early as 1949 and which ends with a recommendation to remember the principle "hold to Christ, and for the rest be totally uncommitted". Looking back in old age I realize that that idea has guided me through life, and although I would now express it differently, that is essentially where I stand.

By the time I left university I had at least made a first acquaintance with many of the Christian writers whose thinking is described in this book, though not those who were engaged in the early theological controversies of the church, for the period from the early church and the writing of the New Testament until at least the beginning of the second millennium is generally neglected by historians, and Christian writers often neglect the next five hundred years as well, only getting really interested in developments in Christian thinking when they get to what was believed by Catholics and Protestants (and occasionally the Orthodox as well) in the early sixteenth century. Some gaps needed to be filled in if I wanted to understand how Christian thought had developed to where it is today.

The German tradition of scholarship, including the study of theology, had survived Nazism, and as a young man I was surprised to find that most modern writings about Christianity which appeared to be worth reading had been written by Germans, or else by theologians of German origin. I had acquired an interest in theology while at university, though my own subject was history, and in my twenties was impressed by what I read about the work of a number of modern theologians, all of them Protestants, and all of them either German or German Americans, whose thinking was influenced perhaps more than anything else by the events of the Nazi era from 1933 until 1945.

Meanwhile, as my knowledge of German history developed, I was acutely aware of the tragedy that the nation of Martin Luther, of Bach, Beethoven and Brahms, of Goethe and Schiller, Kant and Schopenhauer should in the twentieth century have turned to militarism and barbarism on such a massive scale, and it also seemed something of a miracle that out of that horror should have grown a rich flowering of new theological thinking.

My main concerns in the 1960s were my own family life and the teaching of history, but there were three books about Christianity which I was glad to read then and which had a considerable influence on me. The first, by J.S. Whale, a Congregational minister and theologian, was *Christian Doctrine*, which I bought in September 1959, the month after I was married, and which was based on lectures he had given in Cambridge in the autumn of 1940. The second was *Introducing the Christian Faith* by Michael Ramsey, published in 1961, the year in which he became Archbishop of Canterbury and in which at the beginning he declares himself to be a Christian humanist. The third was *Honest to God* by John Robinson, the Bishop of Woolwich, published in 1963.

Robinson explains in the preface the need for a radical recasting of theology, with traditional ideas of, for example, God, the supernatural and religion itself needing to be re-examined, and he goes on to expound some of the thinking of Paul Tillich and Dietrich Bonhoeffer. Some Christians, wanting to cling to the old certainties, reacted to the book with distaste. Others, with me among them, found it comforting and reassuring.

By then I had been a schoolmaster ever since coming down from university in 1957, and most of my reading for the next twenty years was related to the history I was teaching. It was, of course, not primarily about religion, but one could hardly teach *The Crusades* as an A level special subject without knowing something of Catholic and Orthodox Christianity, and Sunni and Shi'ite Islam as well. Similarly, it was necessary when teaching *The Age of Cromwell* to have some understanding of Calvinism and of Arminianism. The short-lived double A level, *History with Foreign Texts,* introduced me to the theological ideas of Anselm of Aosta, and even modern A level special subjects, such as *The French Revolution* and *The Russian Revolutions* required an understanding of why revolutionaries saw not only the monarchy but also the Christian church as something they needed to overthrow.

I continued throughout my life as a member of the Church of England, above all because I saw, and still see, the church as an institution dedicated to keeping alive the things concerning Jesus, even though, being made up of fallible human beings, it often does it inadequately and even badly. As life went by, I became more and more of the opinion that many priests and ministers paid too much attention to telling their congregations what they should believe and too little to explaining how the teaching of Jesus is relevant today – how we should look at things and how we should behave. Some clergy even suggested that, if it had not been for his resurrection and subsequent ascension, Jesus would simply be one more forgotten holy man, whose teaching was in no way more remarkable than that of many others. It seemed to me that they were seriously wrong. Jesus's teaching was revolutionary in its own time, and it still has the power to transform the lives of people who encounter it.

Of course, there have been other great teachers who have also left an enduring impact on mankind. One of the most important in our own civilization, if I may call it that, is Socrates, who died about four hundred years before Jesus was born. Like Jesus he was condemned to death because his ideas were upsetting to those in authority. Like Jesus he went to his death when he could have avoided it, but, also like Jesus, he declined to do so. His influence on succeeding generations is incalculable. Others, notably the Buddha, Confucius and Muhammad, have also transformed millions of lives, and in writing about Christian thinking I in no way wish to disparage them. But I grew up in, and have lived my whole life in, an at least nominally Christian society, and it is about how Christian thinking developed over the last two thousand years that I wish to write.

In retirement my reading has ranged widely and included fiction, biography and philosophy, with each of them probably occupying more of my time than theology. Among philosophical writings it was the work of Bryan Magee, the quintessential apologist for agnosticism, which influenced me most. But a number of books about Christianity caught my attention. One of the earliest, published in 1998, was *Why Christianity Must Change or Die,* by the former Bishop of Newark in the USA, John Shelby Spong. Another was *Doubts and Loves: What Is left of Christianity* by the former bishop of Edinburgh, Richard Holloway, published in 2001. Then in 2003 the American Professor Marcus Borg produced *The Heart of Christianity, Rediscovering a Life of*

Faith, and in the same year a Baptist minister, Steve Chalke, produced *The Lost Message of Jesus.*

I would recommend each of those books, as well as those I mentioned earlier by Professor Butterfield, Archbishop Ramsey and Bishop John Robinson. All seven of those authors were in a sense tackling what they saw as current problems with Christianity. Each of them wrote much else, and in their various different ways they all, of course, knew far more than I do about both theology and biblical criticism. I have no wish to venture into the areas on which they are authorities. So I will not express an opinion about, for example, how far the events surrounding the birth of Jesus that are described in the gospels can be seen as factually accurate, or whether the account given by Matthew or that given by Luke is the more reliable. Nor will I presume to offer an opinion about which is the most helpful of the descriptions by the four evangelists of the events surrounding the crucifixion of Jesus.

Instead of that I hope to show how Christian thinking shifted over the centuries from the teaching of Jesus to where we are now. The first two chapters provide a summary of the thinking of Jesus as described in the gospels and in the letters of some of his followers. The next nine are an account of the how the ideas of leading Christian thinkers developed, and the final chapter attempts an assessment of where the various Christian churches stand today, what the issues are that divide them and how far they are in agreement.

A few years ago, I wrote a short history of the Christian church called *In the Context of Eternity.* In that I attempted to show how the intermingling of Christianity and barbarism on the ruins of the Roman Empire eventually produced the modern world, with its scientific and technological revolutions, capitalism and liberal democracy all co-existing with the Christian church. It involved explaining how the Christian church interacted with and was influenced by political developments. Inevitably Christian thinking and theological ideas intruded into it, but they were not the core of the book. In this book, which can be seen as a companion volume, they are absolutely central, and just as Christian thinking and theology intruded into the former book, so political developments inevitably intrude to some extent into this one. Everything is connected. The way those connections are perceived will vary from one time to another, but one important element of Christianity which has survived down the centuries is the idea that Christians should follow both Jesus's teaching and his example. That idea was given expression in the fifteenth century by Thomas à Kempis in his book *De Imitatione Christi*, and it was given new life near the end of the nineteenth century by an American Congregationalist minister, the Reverend Charles Sturgeon, when he preached a number of sermons in which he presented his congregation with a variety of moral problems and asked the question, "What would Jesus Do?"

I cannot remember when I became aware of the acronym WWJD, which stands for the question, "What would Jesus do?", but I do remember thinking that it was good advice about how to resolve difficult problems about how one should behave. If I now go on to suggest that it is not the ideal way to resolve such problems, that is not to disparage it. It is only to suggest that I believe that Jesus was advocating something beyond that.

I eventually came to believe that the process of conversion should for most of us be not so much changing to be more like Jesus, but rather that it should involve us in changing to be closer to what each one of us would ideally be. As the Danish theologian and philosopher Søren Kierkegaard put it in the mid-nineteenth century, "Be that self which one truly is". Then, when faced with a moral problem, we would not need to ask, "What would Jesus do?", but instead would have reached a point in the process of conversion such that we would be able to follow our own instinct.

That does not mean that we could then congratulate ourselves on knowing the "right" answer to moral problems. In the light of our understanding of the teaching of Jesus we should try to decide well. But we may not. We remain fallible human beings who all too easily make mistakes, and we should avoid being too sure that we are right. A difficult balancing act is needed. On the one hand we need to know what we believe to be valuable and important. On the other we need a measure of humility. The sort of belief worth having is something tentative, striving for Truth, seeking for greater understanding, but recognizing that we do not have and are not going to achieve full Truth. The more one knows, the more one realizes how little one understands.

As time went by it increasingly seemed to me that when the BBC rolled out a couple of speakers to debate some moral issue of current interest, the opinions of the Christian protagonist were often further from the teaching of Jesus and less humane than the opinions of the other speaker. I remembered that Marcus Borg had said that many of his students at Oregon State University in the USA, when asked to write a short essay on their impression of Christianity, had written that they saw it as "literalistic, anti-intellectual, self-righteous, judgmental, and bigoted". Too often one or more of those very words characterised what was presented to the public on the BBC as "the Christian view". It felt as if something had gone badly wrong.

There is, I hope, nowhere in this book any suggestion that the various views I have described, however superficially, of a wide range of Christian thinkers over two thousand years should be seen as the Truth. How could they be when those thinkers so often disagree! But I am suggesting that it is worth making the acquaintance with all of those views. Even when two thinkers disagree profoundly, the ideas of each of them can be illuminating, without either of them necessarily being "right". We can learn from ideas we later believe to be mistaken as well as from those we accept.

In any case, Faith is not primarily a matter of believing things, of giving assent to intellectual propositions and asserting that certain historical events actually happened, however implausible that may seem. It is far more a matter of trust, in this case of trusting in the teaching and example of Jesus of Nazareth. It is also a matter of trying, even if inadequately, to live one's life in accordance with that teaching and example. For many people it can be helpful to have the guidance of the church. But in the end, we all have to make our own decisions.

We need, I believe, to acknowledge the grim aspects of nature: the floods and droughts, the earthquakes and forest fires, and the way in which so many creatures, including mankind, prey on each other. We have to face the fact that for many of them it is necessary to behave in that way if they are to survive, and it is not something which makes it easy to believe in a benevolent God who has for some inscrutable reason arranged things that way. We also need to recognise how trivial each of us is in the context of a vast and apparently impersonal universe. But it is also possible to seek to live one's life aware of the beauty of so much around us and to respond to it. The Germans have a word for this attitude. They speak of someone being *lebensbejaend* (life-be-yes-ing).

Ideally (and, of course, it is not possible for everyone) faithful Christians reach the end of life not worrying over whether they believe enough of the right things to be granted "salvation", but instead feeling grateful that they have had a rich and full life. After all, Jesus is recorded in the tenth chapter of John's gospel as explaining the purpose of his ministry in the words, "I have come that men may have life and may have it abundantly". Then they may be able to look forward to death (though not necessarily to dying) with confidence in the assurance of Jesus that there are many resting places in his Father's house.

Horace, a Roman poet who lived in the century before the life of Christ, may have seen the point when he wrote in one of his odes

(Book III, xxix), the following two stanzas, which were translated into English in the seventeenth century by John Dryden:

Happy the man, and happy he alone,
He who can call today his own.
He who, secure within, can say,
Tomorrow do thy worst, for I have lived today.

Be fair or foul or rain or shine,
The joys I have possessed, in spite of fate, are mine.
Not heaven itself upon the past has power,
But what has been has been, and I have had my hour.

Anyone who is committed to the view that it is essential for Christians to believe a number of theological propositions and that to deny or question them is to err into heresy might prefer to read no further. But someone who is prepared to consider the possibility that what Jesus taught and the way he went to his death are more important than theological propositions could well find it interesting to read on and discover something of how the Christian church has moved over two thousand years from seeking to follow the teaching and example of Jesus to where we are today.

I am not suggesting that Christians should abandon theology, which is the study not just of God but also of religious beliefs. On the contrary, I believe that ideally Christians would know enough of theology and of biblical criticism, and even of ecclesiastical history, to be able to stand up to those who are sure that they are right about their beliefs and demand conformity. Ideally, they will combine a healthy dose of scepticism and even agnosticism with above all valuing "the words of Jesus and his sacrifice".

David Arnold. Summer 2023

Chapter 1

Jesus of Nazareth

A story is told in the gospels of both Mark and Matthew of a meeting between Jesus of Nazareth and a woman whom Mark tells us was Syrophoenician by birth, while Matthew calls her a Canaanite. She came to Jesus begging for help for her daughter who was in great distress. The disciples did not want her pestering Jesus. She was, after all, both a woman and a gentile. Brought up as they were on the assumptions of their people at that time, they assumed that she was not worth bothering about.

Jesus, a Jewish man who had grown up among those same assumptions, tells her that his mission is only to the lost sheep of Israel. When she kneels at his feet and again asks for help, he now says that it is not right to take the children's food and give it to the dogs. By implication she is one of the dogs. But she persists and points out that "even the dogs live on the scraps that fall from their master's table". Jesus accepts what is, however politely put, a rebuke, acknowledges her faith, her trust in him, and, we are told "at that moment her daughter was cured".

It is a much neglected story. After all, Jesus, whom Christians widely believe to have been perfect, was being taught by someone who was both a woman and a gentile that his mission was not just to "the lost sheep of Israel" but to all mankind. It is a crucial moment. No wonder it is included in two of the gospels! And no wonder, in the light of the way the Christian Church developed, that it has often been neglected and ignored! But in that story one can see Jesus growing in wisdom and stature – not God masquerading as a man, but a man who came to be seen as revealing the likeness of God in his own being. One can see his thinking, his view of things, developing.

The Christian religion is based on stories about Jesus. The stories about the events surrounding his birth are told in two of the gospels. Matthew, who is above all concerned to show how they involve a fulfilment of ancient prophecies, narrates them briefly, while Luke, who is above all concerned to proclaim that something wonderful had happened, tells the story in a different way and in far greater detail. Then, near the end of their accounts, all four of the evangelists, Matthew, Mark, Luke and John, describe the events surrounding Jesus's crucifixion. Besides that, there are, spread through the gospels, stories describing his ministry and recounting what he said and what he did.

It is the accounts of what Jesus is reputed to have said that are particularly relevant in a book about Christian thinking, because they reveal what he thought and what he believed to be important. The stories about his life and death and what he did, important though they are, are relevant here only in so far as they reveal his thinking. Before considering them it is worth looking at what he said about how people should behave and about how they should think, and also at the stories he told, at the answers he gave to questions, at what we are told about his praying, and at the instructions he gave to his followers.

Before that it may be worth considering a brief extract from the Revelation of St John the Divine, the extraordinary psychedelic vision written by a prisoner on a Roman penal colony on the island of Patmos late in the first century after the birth of Jesus. Very near the beginning of the Revelation its author describes how he saw "one like a son of man, robed down to his feet, with a golden girdle round his breast. The hair of his head was white as snow-white wool, and his eyes flamed like fire; his feet gleamed like burnished brass refined in a furnace, and his voice was like the sound of rushing waters. In his right hand he held seven stars, and out of his mouth came a sharp two-edged sword; and his face shone like the sun in full strength".

That is an example of something written in Greek by a person who naturally thought in either classical Hebrew or ordinary day to day Aramaic, the language which Jesus usually spoke. It is nothing like the Greek language of philosophers such as Plato or Aristotle, with abstract words conveying subtle differences of meaning. Hebrew and Aramaic are languages in which meaning is conveyed by visual imagery – not words like "omniscient", "omnipotent", "transcendent" or "numinous", but instead, "In his right hand he held seven stars, and out of his mouth came a sharp two-edged sword; and his face shone like the sun in full strength". That visual imagery either will, or perhaps will not, enable you to understand what the author, a different John from the apostle, is getting at.

The language Jesus uses is not the overblown, colourful, exotic language of the Revelation of St John the Divine. It is far more down to earth and far more readily accessible. It is nevertheless the language of someone who, like any Jew of his day, naturally expressed himself in visual imagery and did not have at his disposal the abstract language of Greek philosophers. A good example of his use of visual imagery is given at the end of the twenty-fifth chapter of Matthew's gospel.

We read that Jesus told his listeners that when the Son of Man comes in glory, surrounded by angels and seated on a throne of glory, he will separate people as a shepherd separates sheep from goats, and he will welcome the sheep into his kingdom and cast the goats into eternal fire. The former he thanks for such things as feeding him when hungry, clothing him when naked, and visiting him when ill. When they do not understand, he explains that inasmuch as they did it to one of the least of his brethren, they did it for him. Similarly, he tells the others that inasmuch as they had not helped one of the least of those brethren, they had failed to help him.

We need to ask ourselves whether the description by Jesus, of those on the right hand entering the Kingdom of Heaven and those on the left being consigned to eternal punishment in fire, is a prediction of what will happen on the Day of Judgement, or an assertion with vivid visual imagery that there really is an important difference between good and bad behaviour? Too often preachers have proclaimed the former, misleading their congregations about the significance of Jesus's message because they did not realise how Jesus was using visual imagery.

That story raises the question of what Jesus thought about the Kingdom of Heaven, which he also speaks about as the Kingdom of God. It is something he seems to have commented on quite often. Luke tells us that he was asked by some Pharisees when it would come, and he replied that it never comes by watching for it. "Men cannot say, 'Look here it is' or 'There it is', for the Kingdom of God is within you". He also told them that it was "among you" and "near you". That is, Jesus asserts quite clearly that the Kingdom of Heaven is a spiritual kingdom around us and within us, and not a place up in the sky inhabited by angels.

Matthew also tells us that Jesus tried to explain the idea of heaven by saying that it was like a tiny grain of mustard seed, which could grow into a tree, so that all the birds of the air could come and lodge in its branches. Or again, he suggested that it was like yeast in its transforming effect. It should be possible, even for us, two thousand years later, in a society in which we seldom use visual imagery the way he did, to avoid interpreting his words literally and instead understand what he meant.

A particularly famous account of his teaching is given in the fifth chapter of Matthew's gospel, in what is referred to as the Sermon on the Mount. On that occasion he proclaimed to his followers the value of humility, of experiencing suffering, of being undemanding, concerned for goodness, kind, pure in heart, peaceable, and even suffering persecution because of one's concern for what is good and right. He stressed that he had no intention of seeking to overthrow the Law. On the contrary, he wanted to show how it could be fulfilled. He was advocating an ideal of perfection which went beyond what was required by the Law. Thus, while the Law, of course, forbad murder and required that "anyone who commits murder must be brought to judgement", Jesus said that anyone who was angry with his brother should be brought to judgement. "If he sneers at him, he will have to answer for it in the fires of hell".

That is something which his listeners would have understood better than many people today, because nowadays many people, however literate, have little understanding of how the language which Jesus spoke was used, and some will think that Jesus was proclaiming that hell-fire is the literal and necessary consequence of sneering. As late as the twenty-first century there are still those who regret the passing of hell-fire preaching, as if the lack of it is an indication of the way the essential Christian message has been watered down. But that is to miss the point of Jesus's teaching. He was telling his listeners how they should view things and how they should live their lives and was using visual imagery to make forcibly the point that some ways of behaving are good and others are bad. At the end of Matthew's gospel we are told that Jesus commanded his followers to go out and make disciples of all the nations: "Teach them to observe all that I have commanded you". He was not telling them what they should believe. He was telling them what they should do.

He was not setting down a new set of rules to be obeyed, still less setting out appropriate punishments for disobeying, such as designating a given number of years, or even an eternity, of hell-fire to anyone who calls his brother a fool. He was teaching them how to live, not in the sense of obeying rules, however necessary that may be, but rather by adopting a new way of looking at things, with higher standards than the Law, which was to him and his listeners the first five books of the Old Testament. Those five books, when gathered together, were referred to as the Law. That Law, in Exodus chapter 20 verse 14, condemns committing adultery; Jesus demands that men should not even look at a woman with lust. The Law, in Leviticus chapter 19 verse 18, requires that you should love your neighbour; Jesus requires you to love even your enemy.

At the same time, he told his followers not to be ostentatious about their goodness, and to be prepared to forgive those who make mistakes. A life spent seeking to do good is more worthwhile than one devoted to making money. His followers should not be too quick to criticize other people if they do not want to be criticized themselves. Talking about one's devotion to God is all very well, but what matters is doing what is right, not talking about it. He sums up his teaching with the words, "Treat other people exactly as you would like to be treated yourself. This is the essence of true religion". Nowadays that is often referred to as the Golden Rule.

Jesus did not demand changes in the Law and he invented no new rules. But he did tell his followers that they should aim to "be perfect, even as your Father in Heaven is perfect", and Luke tells us in the fifth chapter of his gospel that Jesus said, "You must be kind, as your father in heaven is kind. Don't judge others and you will not be judged yourself. Don't condemn and you will not be condemned. Make allowances for others and they will make allowances for you". He clearly regarded the way people behave as more important than what they say. Thus, he told his disciples, "It is not everyone who keeps saying to me 'Lord, Lord' who will enter the Kingdom of Heaven, but the man who actually does my heavenly father's will".

Jesus, as much as any other Jewish man of his time, appreciated the value of the Sabbath as a day of rest on which men could particularly devote themselves to the worship of God. But he was entirely out of sympathy with a strict legalistic interpretation of how one should behave on the Sabbath. When his disciples were criticized by some Pharisees for picking ears of corn as they walked through cornfields on the Sabbath, on the grounds that that constituted working on the Sabbath,

Jesus told them that "the Sabbath was made for man, not man for the Sabbath". When, hoping that his answer would enable them to bring a charge against him, they asked if it was right to heal anyone on the Sabbath, he in return asked them if they would not pull out a sheep which had fallen into a ditch on the Sabbath. The same, he was suggesting, applies to caring for one's fellows on the Sabbath, and he went ahead with his work of healing.

Very often his teaching took the form of telling stories – stories which we call parables. Some are well known. The story of the Good Samaritan is particularly well known and is clearly intended to indicate the difference between good and bad behaviour and attitudes. This story, about a man who fell among thieves, was intended to upset normal expectations. The requirements of the Law for ritual cleansing after contact with the dead made it difficult for pious Jews to touch a body lying by the wayside, and the person who eventually helps the man who fell among thieves is a Samaritan.

At the time Jews viewed the Samaritans with distaste as Israelites who lived in the territory to the North of Jerusalem which had once been part of the Kingdom of Israel, had intermarried with Gentiles, neglected the Temple in Jerusalem, and had betrayed the faith of their fathers. That a Samaritan is the hero of the story upset assumptions, and it is difficult nowadays, when we think of Samaritans as kindly people who listen to others in distress, to appreciate quite how much it upset those assumptions. Jesus, as a particularly good teacher, left his listeners to work out the implications for themselves.

Just what people learn from Jesus's parables depends on their own circumstances, their culture and, indeed, their own cast of mind. What is remarkable is the extent to which so many of the stories have applicability centuries later and what depth and different meanings can be found in them. This is demonstrably so in the case of the story known as the Parable of the Prodigal

Son about a young man who "wasted his substance in riotous living", became destitute and returned home penitent.

In the late twentieth century a Roman Catholic priest, Henri Nouwen, feeling homeless and tired, looked at Rembrandt's picture of *The Return of the Prodigal Son*, in which the prodigal is kneeling as his father embraces him, while the elder brother is standing resentfully by. Nouwen identified strongly with the prodigal son, longing to be somehow welcomed home. But when he explained to a friend how he felt, the friend replied, "I wonder if you are not more like the elder brother". It shook him. Much later he told all this to another old friend, who replied, "Whether you are the younger or the elder son, you have to realise that you are called to become the father". So in 1986 he went to work in a community which looked after mentally disabled people and died there ten years later.

A third particularly well-known story that Jesus told is of two men who went up to the temple to pray, the one a Pharisee, and the other a publican – that is, not an inn-keeper but a public official who collected taxes for the Roman occupying forces. The Pharisee thanked God that he was not like so many other men, who extorted money from the poor, were unjust, and committed adultery. He took pride in the fact that he fasted twice a week and gave away a tenth of everything he possessed, and he was thankful that he was not like the nearby publican. Meanwhile, the publican would not even lift up his eyes, but instead said, "God be merciful to me, a sinner". Jesus tells us that it was this man who went down to his house justified, that is, in a right relationship with God, rather than the other.

This story, probably more than any other, gets over the point which mattered so much to Jesus that, even though what you do matters more than what you say, ultimately what matters most is your attitude of mind. The Pharisee was not greedy or dishonest or adulterous. One can assume that he was telling the truth about his behaviour. But he was pleased with himself and saw himself as virtuous – and that won't do, as far as Jesus was concerned.

At the time the way Jesus looked at things was novel and very upsetting, and his teaching gave such offence that the leaders of the Jewish church began to look for ways to silence him. It remains a problem today, for Christians who may well spend their lives seeking to follow Christ can sometimes look suspiciously like the Pharisee. There is probably an element of both the Pharisee and the publican in most of us. We should try, as Jesus commanded, to be perfect, "even as your Father in Heaven is perfect", but at the same time recognise that we are going to fall far short of the ideal of perfection, and avoid feeling too pleased with ourselves.

Other parables appear to have been aimed at teaching his followers how to view life realistically. The parable about the labourers in the vineyard, in which those who had worked only for a short while were paid as much as those who had worked for hours through the heat of the day, makes the point that life is not fair. The parable of the talents, in which the person with only one talent has it taken from him and given to a man who had had ten and made good use of them, makes the point that life is hard for the weak and also that people should make good use of such talents as they have. In the original story a talent was a coin of some value, and the modern meaning of the word is a tribute to the power of the original story.

Jesus also told his followers to "repent", which is often represented as meaning "be sorry for what you have done wrong", and, of course, he told his listeners to make peace with anyone with whom they have a grievance. But the Greek word *metanoeite*, which is usually translated as "repent", means something more like "think differently" or "change your hearts", and it involves the idea that those who follow Jesus should be committed to conversion of life. He was teaching that they should adopt a different way of looking at things, and that point about both looking at things differently and behaving differently is made in a story which is told both by Luke and John.

Fairly early in Luke's gospel we are told that Jesus tells Simon to push out into deep water and let down his nets for a catch – and they "caught an enormous shoal of fish, so big that the nets began to tear". At that point it looks as if the main point of the story lies in Jesus's comment to Simon afterwards that "from now on you will be catching men", and the story ends, after Simon and his partners, James and John, have got the boats ashore, with all three of them leaving everything to follow Jesus.

Much the same story turns up again near the end of John's gospel – after the crucifixion and the resurrection. This time Simon, now also known as Peter, or Rocky, together with one or two other disciples, had again been fishing all night without catching anything, when the resurrected Jesus appears and tells them to throw the net in on the other side. They do, and this time, when they drag the net to land, it is full of big fish, a hundred and fifty-three of them – and "the net was not torn". Now it is clearly the same story, even if this time the net was not torn. So it is worth asking why John thought it worth putting there.

The answer, very probably, is that it was central to Jesus's teaching that his followers should look at things differently and behave differently. There is little point in our agonizing over whether or not much the same thing could have happened twice. The important thing is to try to see the point of the story and why it matters – not whether Luke or John is right about damage to the nets and whether it happened at the beginning of Jesus's ministry or after the resurrection. It is also an example of Jesus teaching by getting his disciples to do something. He appreciated how easy it is to forget what one is told.

Quite often in the gospels one can see what Jesus was thinking by considering his answers to questions. Mark tells us that a lawyer asked Jesus "Which commandment is first of all?" His reply was not a reference to Exodus, in which can be found the first of the ten commandments of Moses (*I am the Lord thy God, which have brought thee out of the land of Egypt, out of the house of bondage. Thou shalt have no other gods before me*), but instead he selects the fifth and sixth verses of the sixth chapter of Deuteronomy (*Hear, O Israel: The Lord thy God is one Lord, and thou shalt love the Lord thy God with all thy heart, with all thy soul, and with all thy might*), and he comments, "This is the first commandment, and the second is like, namely this: *Thou shalt love thy neighbour as thyself*", adding, "There is none other commandment greater than these". What he describes as the second commandment are words from verse eighteen of chapter nineteen of Leviticus.

Clearly Jesus knew his way around the scriptures. He had the authority which comes from knowing his subject. The lawyer who asked the question was impressed by the answer Jesus gave him and says that he is absolutely right, adding that to love God and one's neighbours is "more than all burnt offerings and sacrifices". Jesus tells him that he is not far from the kingdom of God.

Sometimes we are given an insight into Jesus's thinking when we hear how he responded to criticism. When some Pharisees criticised his disciples for not washing their hands properly before eating, in accordance with Jewish custom, he told them that it was the thoughts that arise in a man's mind, such as murder, adultery, theft, perjury and blasphemy, which make him unclean, not eating without washing his hands properly.

Some Pharisees also asked him if it was right for a man to divorce his wife. He responds by asking them what the Law of Moses says, knowing, of course, that it indicates that a man may indeed do so. Then he tells them that Moses gave them that commandment because men understand so little of love, and he tells his disciples that a man who divorces his wife and marries another commits adultery against his wife. He was not suggesting that the law permitting divorce should be overthrown. He was asserting that ideally the man would love his wife and not treat her as a chattel to be lightly thrown away.

They also brought before him a woman caught in the act of adultery and, knowing that the Law said that she should be stoned to death, asked what he thought should be done. His answer was that whoever had never sinned should cast the first stone. They all went away, and Jesus said to her, "Neither do I condemn you. Go, and do not sin again". It is worth noticing that the man with whom she committed adultery was not accused, and also that again Jesus did not reject the law. But he showed how inappropriate it had become.

They were living in a country in which many were resentful of Roman occupation, so the Pharisees tried to trap him with the question of whether or not it was right to pay taxes to Caesar. It looked as if one answer would get him into trouble with the Roman authorities, while the other would seem a betrayal to his followers. He asked to see a coin and then asked whose face was on it. The answer, of course, was "Caesar's". "So", he said, "Give to Caesar what belongs to Caesar and to God what belongs to God". It was not just a clever answer. It also makes the important point that he was not concerned with overthrowing any particular system of government but rather with people behaving in a sensible and appropriate fashion.

Jesus's teaching was about how we should live our lives, and even more about how we should look at things, and one consequence of that is that we perpetually need to examine our own behaviour and motivation and reflect on how far we manage to live according to his teaching. It is not just a matter of what we do. It is also a matter of our attitude of mind. He offers a council of perfection, and he tells us that what matters most is getting our relationships right, with God and with the people around us – not just our friends but everyone.

He had no aspiration to overthrow the Law. He knew that human societies need law. But getting one's relationships right with God and one's fellows is not a matter of meticulous obedience to the Law. So he was critical of those who were so scrupulous in their obedience to the Law that, in their zeal to pay tithes, they cut a tenth part off every leaf of each herb they were using, but meanwhile neglected the justice and the love of God.

If we want to live a good life, we need to recognise that it is not a matter of obeying rules, however much it is on the whole desirable that one should do so. Rather it is a matter of understanding the teaching of Jesus and following his guidance. Near the end of his ministry, and knowing what is coming, Jesus told his close followers to set their troubled hearts at rest, to trust in God and trust in him. He told them that there were many resting places in his Father's house, that he was going there to prepare a place for them, and that his way there is known to them. Thomas protested that they do not know the way, and Jesus replied, "I am the Way, the Truth and the Life". He went on: "No one comes to the Father except by me".

He was reiterating what he had so often told them before: that it is not by meticulous obedience to the Law that they will get into a right relationship with God but rather by following both his own example and his teaching. It is a saying which needs to be seen in the context of Thomas's question. It is not an assertion that anyone who does not know of him or who follows some other religion is necessarily excluded from the love of God. It is a reply to Thomas, entirely in line with what he has been teaching throughout his ministry. We all fall short. If we want to do better, we should follow his teaching and his example. That is the way to get into a right relationship with God.

When we look at the example of his behaviour towards those referred to in English translations of the Bible as lepers and towards other outcasts of society, it is all the easier to understand what he was teaching. What he did spoke even louder than the words he used. There is a story in John's gospel of how, near the end of his ministry, "Jesus, knowing that the Father had given all things into his hands, and that he was come from God, and was going to God, rose from supper, laid aside his garments, took a towel, and girded himself. After that he poured water into a basin and began to wash the disciples' feet". He was teaching his disciples and us about how to live a good life, and he did so by washing their feet.

He washed his disciples' feet first of all because they were dirty and someone needed to clean them. He was also teaching them. "If I then, your Lord and Master", he said, "have washed your feet, you also ought to wash one another's feet". Beyond that it was a symbolic gesture that his mission was to wash humankind clean. What is more, when he physically washed the feet of his companions, who, like him, were free, Jewish and men, he stooped down and undertook work reserved for slaves, gentiles and women. He identified himself with all humankind, particularly the poor, the despised and the oppressed. His actions proclaimed that he was there for all who needed him. It is an account of brilliant teaching. It is also an insight into his thinking.

Where Matthew, Mark and Luke all tell of the Last Supper, John gives an account of an extended prayer. It is impossible to know how far John was quoting words he had heard Jesus speak aloud and how far he was trying to convey what he understood Jesus to care about. Either way, it is clear that John saw it as important to convey to his readers that as Jesus went to his death, he was above all concerned with relationships: his own relationship with the Being he thinks of and addresses as Father, his relationship with the disciples, their relationship with the Father, and their relationships with each other. It is clear that those relationships should be expressions of love.

Jesus was eventually crucified as a common criminal because he had offended the religious leaders of the Jews. They saw his teaching and in particular his criticisms of their attitudes as a threat. He had even overturned the tables of money-changers and traders in the Temple, saying that a place of prayer had been turned into a den of thieves. It was too much. The Jewish religious leaders suggested to the Roman governor of Judea that Jesus was a threat to him as well, and was setting himself up as a king. Jesus then went to the cross because he would not change his teaching for fear of the consequences.

He was not seeking conflict. Instead, he was teaching a doctrine of Love summed up in the Golden Rule that people should treat others as they would wish to be treated themselves. But at the same time, he was critical of the way many Pharisees and experts in the Law behaved, and he would not tone down his criticism in order to save his own skin. He had taught that those who were persecuted for the sake of righteousness were blessed. Now he was in that position himself. There were worse things than death, he believed, and one such thing was betraying the cause of righteousness. He was not seeking death, but he would not say or do anything contrary to his beliefs in order to avoid it.

For the next two thousand years Christians argued about why he was crucified, and in the middle of the nineteenth century four very different views were beautifully summarised by Mrs C.F. Alexander, the wife of the Bishop of Derry, in a famous hymn. The words of the third verse are: "He died that we might be forgiven, he died to make us good, that we might go at last to heaven, saved by his precious blood". Each of those statements illustrates the way some Christians have over the centuries thought about the crucifixion, and the hymn ends: "O, dearly, dearly has he loved, and we must love him too, and trust in his redeeming love, and try his works to do". None of those views of the crucifixion involves the idea of an angry Father, with the Son suffering while the Holy Spirit is ignored. But one much-proclaimed modern idea is that God was so angry with the sins of mankind that He punished His innocent son, Jesus, instead of the rest of mankind, who were all guilty. It is as if the head teacher of a school, cross with the misbehaviour of the children in the school, went home and killed her own innocent and well-behaved child. It makes God sound psychotic. But it regularly crops up in Christendom in Holy Week and does immense damage.

Those who preach such unpleasant nonsense seem not to consider how many people they turn away from Christ. They seek to convert them, but instead drive untold numbers away. Somehow, a religion which began with promoting the thinking and example of Jesus, shifted over the centuries to one in which it is possible to promote the idea that God caused Jesus to die in agony as a substitute for sinful mankind – and this despite the fact that John tells us in the tenth chapter of his gospel that Jesus said quite explicitly that no one was robbing him of his life: "I lay it down of my own free will".

Chapter 2

Four Apostles: Paul, James, Peter and John

Jesus warned his disciples that his way of looking at things was liable to get them into trouble, and it did. At the end of the seventh chapter of the Acts of the Apostles we hear of the stoning to death of Stephen, the first Christian martyr, and at the same time we hear that a young Pharisee with the proud, royal name of Saul was "among those who approved of his murder". Saul afterwards "made havoc of the church", hauling many of the disciples off to prison. One consequence of this was that the church spread further, because the disciples fled from Jerusalem to other towns, and before long Saul, "breathing out threatenings and slaughter against the disciples of the Lord", set off to destroy the Christian church in Damascus.

The story of the conversion of Saul on the road to Damascus is well known. He experienced a bright flashing light, fell to the ground, heard a voice speaking to him and was blind for three days afterwards. A modern psychiatrist would probably suggest that he had what is known as an hysterical personality and had had a near death experience. Whatever it was, it transformed his life. He was new-born into the Christian community, adopted a new and humble name, Paul (*Paulus* in Latin means "little" or "small"), and set out to convert the world. By proclaiming the Good News of Christ to the Gentiles, with its message of the importance of trusting in Jesus rather than in conscientious obedience to the Law, and at the same time preaching the importance of forgiveness and reconciliation, he helped to transform the course of History.

It is the only instance in the Bible of that sort of conversion. It is not the way the lives of most of Jesus's followers are changed. But the story illustrates dramatically what are frequently the

31

characteristics of Christian conversion. First, something was wrong. Secondly, Saul turned to Jesus as his Lord and Saviour (Acts chapter 9 verse 20). Thirdly, he became a member of the Christian community. Finally, he spent his life using the talents which God had given him, and which in his case were remarkable, in the service of his Lord.

He believed that it was his mission to explain the significance of Jesus's death and resurrection to the Gentiles and to pass on Jesus's teaching to them. The infrastructure of the Roman Empire, its roads and shipping routes, enabled him to travel relatively easily through Syria, Asia Minor and Greece and eventually to Rome, and whenever he came to a new town he would start by teaching in the synagogue. He was preaching the idea that all human beings, Jews and Gentiles alike, male and female, slave and free, should follow Christ's teaching and example. The result of this was often that Paul was driven from the synagogue, after which he would seek to build up a Christian community somewhere else in the town, and later would keep in touch by letters.

Some of those letters are among our very earliest Christian documents – earlier than the gospels, which are often mistakenly thought to have been written earlier because they are printed at the beginning of the collection of documents known as the New Testament. All of them, the letters and the gospels, are written in Koine Greek, or "common Greek", a very different language from classical Greek, and the common tongue in the eastern Mediterranean at that time, thus making them far more accessible to a wide range of people than if they had been written in Aramaic, the local language of their authors.

So significant is the work of Paul, his evangelizing and the letters which followed up his early contacts, that he is sometimes credited with being the founder of Christianity. If it hadn't been for him, it is suggested, the message of Jesus would gradually have faded until it was forgotten. But History is about what did happen rather than about what might have happened, and what happened was that Paul's mission was very influential. He spread Jesus's teaching, preaching a gospel of love to all humankind and exhorting Christians to avoid empty rites and ceremonies when they should be concentrating on the new way of looking at things taught by Jesus, concentrating on love of God and one's neighbour, on forgiveness and reconciliation, and living a life characterized by such things as humility, kindness and a concern for peace.

Paul's great achievement was to establish that it was faith, or trust, in God rather than obedience to the Law which was needed for salvation. The conservative view was that the basis for salvation was obedience to God's commandments as set out in the Mosaic Law. Paul, in contradiction to that, argued that Jesus had made it clear that no one could acquire salvation, or get into a right relationship with God, by obedience to the Law and by good works. All were guilty and in need of forgiveness. What was needed was for men to recognise their own sinfulness and seek the divine forgiveness which Jesus had promised. Once this right relationship with God was established, once Christians were at one with God, that should lead them on to perform "good works". But those works would be the consequence of getting into a right relationship with God, not the means by which that relationship was achieved. It was Paul who established this fundamental element of Christian teaching: that good works are the fruit of salvation, not the price paid for it.

It is essential to bear in mind that Paul, like Jesus, was a Jewish man of the first century, with all the religious, cultural and social assumptions of his time, and not only that. He was one of the sect known as Pharisees about whom Jesus had been particularly critical because so many of them were meticulous about obeying every detail of the Law rather than caring for justice and the love of God.

It is also important to remember that his letters were written not for posterity, with every word carefully weighed, but rather to particular people, such as Timothy or Titus or Philemon, or to groups, such as the Christians in Thessalonica or Galatia, and he was often dealing with particular problems. Thus, in one of his earliest letters, the second one to the Christians at Thessalonica, he reminds them that he had left them with the principle that "if a man will not work, he shall not eat". That is not a general principle which can be used two thousand years later to justify cutting unemployment benefit to starvation level. It relates to the immediate problem that some early Christians were sitting around doing nothing except waiting for the Second Coming of Christ in glory. Paul was telling them that that would not do.

Although at an early stage in his ministry he seems to have believed that Jesus might at any moment come again in glory, he soon moved to the idea that Christ is, was, and ever will be present within the church. The truth embodied in Jesus's message about love and reconciliation, Paul suggested, did not depend on whether the world ended sooner or later. It is an eternal truth. The church continues in time, embraces all believers, and unites all Christians through the sacraments of baptism and the eucharist (*eucharistia* is a Greek word which means "thanksgiving") and through shared faith in the Lord. The central message of Paul's letters is consistently that faith, or trust, in the Lord is what matters, rather than conscientious obedience to the Law of Moses.

"The Law kills, but the spirit gives life", he wrote in the second of his letters to the Christians at Corinth. But that is not a simple, straightforward assertion which solves all problems, and Paul was writing to them because the belief seems to have spread in Corinth that all material things are evil and everything immaterial is good. That belief led some to interpret the Pauline doctrine of freedom from the Law as a justification for lust and self-indulgence, while at the other extreme it led others into extremes of asceticism. It was to combat tendencies such as these that Paul wrote this second letter to the Corinthians.

It is clear in that letter, when he addresses this problem, that he is writing to a particular group for a particular reason and was not writing a treatise intended to be guidance for all people at all time. But the fact that similar problems have gone on arising down the ages means that, however much his letters were written at a particular time, to a particular group, and to deal with a particular problem, they have far wider applicability. The problem for us lies in discerning what in Paul's writings is ephemeral and what is eternal.

The sixteenth verse of the third chapter of Paul's second letter to Timothy, in the translation known either as the Authorized Version or as the King James Version of the Bible reads: *All scripture is given by inspiration of God, and is profitable for doctrine, for reproof, for correction, for instruction in righteousness.* That is sometimes taken to mean that every verse, every "scripture", has eternal and general applicability. But some of the content of Paul's letters, far from being eternal and of general applicability, is clearly ephemeral. That applies to a request in that same letter to bring him his cloak, which he had "left at Troas with Carpus". It applies to the salutation he gives to Prisca and Aquila, and to his complaint about Alexander the coppersmith. There is also a very personal touch in the advice to Timothy: "Drink no longer water, but use a little wine for thy stomach's sake and thine often infirmities". This is not a truth of universal applicability, so we do not need to feel guilty if we drink orange juice rather than wine.

Some of Paul's advice in his letters to Timothy is more generally applicable but relates to the social circumstances of the first century AD rather than to a distant future. "A woman should learn quietly and humbly", he writes. "Personally, I don't allow women to teach, nor do I ever put them in positions of authority over men – I believe their role is to be receptive". That would be objectionably sexist today, but in the first century AD it was probably sound advice, however fond he was of Prisca and Aquila, about whom, tantalisingly, we know no more than that Paul sends them his love at the end of his second letter to Timothy.

Similarly, the exhortation to Christian slaves to treat their masters with respect should be seen in the context of the first century rather than as an endorsement for all time of the institution of slavery. It is a widespread and common human failing to judge people in the past by the social norms of our own time, and we all need to be able to forgive Paul his views on women and slaves and, indeed, on homosexuals. We need to see him as a Jewish man of the first century AD, both a Pharisee and a Roman citizen, giving sensible and practical guidance, on the one hand in the light of the teaching of Jesus, and on the other in the light of the social norms of the time. He did not want the Christian community brought into disrepute by what might be seen as extravagant and rude behaviour.

Not surprisingly his letters include some wise comments which are as true today as two thousand years ago, such as: "For we brought nothing into the world, and it is certain we can carry nothing out". And shortly after that we read that "the love of money is the root of all evil". That is not entirely right. Bullying and rape, for example, do not usually arise from a love of money. But it is a wise and memorable comment which still resonates today in a society where so many people suffer from the greed of others.

Paul's letters need to be read as real letters written by a human being who had much to say that was worth saying, and not with every phrase seen as the infallible Word of God. Much in them repays thought. Paul tells Timothy "the Law is not made for a righteous man, but for the lawless and disobedient". That is particularly worth thinking about in the light of the words of Jesus: "The Sabbath was made for man, and not man for the Sabbath", and one can add that the scriptures were made for man, and not man for the scriptures.

In his letter to Titus he warns him to "avoid foolish questions and genealogies and contentions and strivings about the law, for they are unprofitable and vain". There are, he is suggesting, books of the Hebrew Scriptures which repay study more than, for example, the opening chapters of the First Book of the Chronicles. In that first book of the Chronicles more than half of the words in the first chapter are either names or the word "and", and it carries on like that for eight more chapters. At the time the record was made it was, no doubt, useful to someone, but its usefulness was lost even by the first century AD.

That brings us back to Paul's comment to Timothy that "all scripture is inspired by God and is profitable for doctrine". The last three words in Greek are *ophelimos pros didaskalian*, and "useful for teaching" is probably a better translation than "profitable for doctrine". That all scripture can be "useful for teaching" remains true two thousand years later. Even the early chapters of Chronicles had once been useful to someone engaged in genealogical research. The opening of the Book of Genesis is a model of how to construct a short descriptive essay. The Book of Joshua shows us how the Children of Israel perceived their tribal god in the days when they entered the Promised Land. The last chapters of the Second Book of the Kings provide a glimpse of an early attempt to get to grips with the problem of causation in history. The books of the prophets Hosea, Amos and Micah show something of how the Hebrew vision of God developed.

There are innumerable such examples, and Paul would, no doubt, have been pleased to know that both the ancient Hebrew scriptures and his own writings are still valued by Christians nearly two thousand years after his death. But that does not mean that every sentence of scripture was dictated by God and that particular texts from Paul's letters can be used as a knock-down argument to justify one's own prejudices.

Paul tells us in the letter to the Galatians that the works of the flesh are "adultery, fornication, uncleanness, lasciviousness, idolatry, witchcraft, hatred, variance, emulations, wrath, strife, seditions, heresies, envying, murders, drunkenness, revelling and such like". Immediately before rattling off that list, he had just said that "if you are led of the Spirit, you are not under the Law". It is important to appreciate that it is not a list of prohibitions, but rather a list of what he saw as the likely consequences of an unsound view of things and the lack of a good relationship with God.

Immediately after that he tells the Galatians that the fruits of the Spirit are "love, joy, peace, long-suffering, gentleness, goodness, faith, meekness, temperance". Again, it is important to appreciate that he is not saying that Christians have an obligation to seek to exhibit those qualities. He is saying that they are the consequence, or fruit, of being led by the Spirit. If you trust in the Lord, if you seek to follow him and do what he asks, if you can look at the world around you as he taught us to, then the consequence is that you will not be angry, drunken, lascivious and so on but rather, depending on the circumstances in which you are living, you will be likely to have a loving, temperate, peaceful and joyful approach to things. That is a very different matter from saying that you are required to present yourself to those around you with a sort of perpetual, compulsory optimism.

Some of the arguments in Paul's letters clearly arise from needing to deal with disagreements about what it meant to be a Christian. In his letter to the Romans, written in about AD 57, and the only one of his letters which reads like a carefully thought out treatise rather than a response to particular circumstances, Paul sets out a long and detailed explanation of his central message, that no one can be "justified" by adherence to the Law. Instead, he claims "it is by faith that we are justified". He insists that "a man is justified by faith quite apart from success in keeping the law".

Similarly, in the letter to the Christians in Galatia, probably written a couple of years earlier, he opens with indignation and self-justification as he condemns those who want to take Christians back to obeying the Mosaic Law and he makes the same point that we are "justified by our faith and not by obedience to the law". The tone of the two letters is entirely different. The teaching is the same.

The difference of tone is significant. In the letter to the Christians in Galatia, Paul criticises them for listening to those who "distort the gospel of Christ". He calls them idiots who seem to have been bewitched. "Answer me one question: did you receive the Spirit by keeping the law or by believing the gospel message? Can it be that you are so stupid?" That is not a carefully thought out reasoned argument. It is the voice of perhaps the greatest evangelist of all time, writing with passion and telling the Galatians what really matters. It is an explosion of passion – and all the better for that. It is far easier to follow than the letter to the Romans.

Before leaving Paul it is worth turning to the passage near the beginning of his letter to the Christians at Rome, in which he lambastes those who, he believes, deliberately turn aside from God and indulge their own disgraceful passions. "Their women exchanged the normal practices of sexual intercourse for something which is abnormal and unnatural. Similarly the men, turning from natural intercourse with women, were swept into lustful passions for one another. Men with men performed these shameful horrors, receiving, of course, in their own personalities the consequences of sexual perversity".

He goes on say that they "became filled with wickedness, rottenness, greed and malice: their minds became steeped in envy, murder, quarrelsomeness, deceitfulness and spite". But then at the beginning of chapter 2 you find him saying, "Now if you feel inclined to set yourself up as a judge of those who sin, let me assure you, whoever you are, that you are in no position to do so".

It is worth seeking an explanation of this. First, it is important to remember that Paul was a Jew of the first century, and a Pharisee at that. He had grown up dedicated to keeping scrupulously to the Law and knew from Leviticus, chapter 18 verse 22 that homosexuality was an abomination, like eating the flesh of a pig, and an explanation worth considering of Paul's subsequent attitude has been put forward as a possibility by a former Bishop of Newark in the USA, Jack Spong.

He suggests that Paul may himself have been by nature homosexual, was deeply ashamed of it, and had in his youth regarded his own nature with abhorrence. That was, perhaps, the thorn in the flesh that he could not get rid of. "The good that I would, I do not", he wrote, "and the evil that I would not, that I do". But in a blinding flash of illumination on the road to Damascus he had realised that Jesus offered forgiveness and salvation even to such as him. That explanation is, of course, no more than a possibility, and, if true, it is not a criticism of Paul, even if it did cause him to think of himself as "the chief of sinners".

One of his greatest achievements was to establish equal status for gentile and Jewish Christians. His view that Christians, whether Jew or gentile, were called to follow Christ rather than being bound by the Mosaic Law was accepted by the other leaders of the church. Both the Acts of the Apostles and Paul's letter to the Christians of Galatia refer to a conference in Jerusalem where the leaders of the Christian church settled a number of matters on which there was disagreement. Traditionalists expected all male gentile converts to be circumcised. Paul did not. Peter, John and James, "the Lord's brother", who seems to have emerged as the leader of the church in Jerusalem, all came down on Paul's side.

These three appear to have contributed much to the development of the early church, and although we know less about their teaching and thinking than that of Paul, because Paul was such a prolific letter writer, their influence was clearly important. James, who should not be confused with the two apostles of that name, one the son of Zebedee and the other the son of Alphaeus, is first met in the Gospels of both Mark and Matthew, when Jesus visits his home town of Nazareth and the people say, "Isn't this the carpenter, the son of Mary, the brother of James and Joseph and Judas and Simon?" Some think of those four brothers as half-brothers of Jesus, because they take the view that, while Jesus was born of Mary and "conceived of the Holy Spirit", James, Joseph, Judas and Simon were the sons of both Mary and Joseph.

In what may be the very earliest letter of the New Testament, written very probably by James, "the Lord's brother", the message to Christian Jews scattered around Asia Minor is that men do not get into a right relationship with God just by declaring their faith. They need not only to understand the will of God but also to put it into practice. True religion, James tells us, is such things as visiting orphans and widows in their distress, and, he says, a man's faith can be judged by his behaviour. James tells his readers that "faith without works is dead", and goes on to say quite explicitly that "by works a man is justified, and not by faith only".

When he writes that the wisdom which comes from God is "first utterly pure, then peace-loving, gentle, approachable, and full of tolerant thoughts and kindly actions", he is echoing the teaching in the Sermon on the Mount, which Matthew later described in his gospel, telling us how Jesus spoke of the merits of humility, kindness and purity, and of the importance of loving peace. James was teaching what he had heard from

Jesus, and he tells his readers that it is a sin to know what is right and fail to do it. That is, he had realised that what were later called sins of omission could be just as important as sins of commission. There is a difference of emphasis in his teaching from that of Paul, but, essentially, they are agreed, and they are both echoing the teaching of Jesus, that faith, or trust in his teaching and example, are more important than meticulous conformity to the Law, but also that that faith should bear fruit in living a good life and doing good works.

Peter, one of the apostles who was particularly close to Jesus, also wrote to Jews dispersed through Asia Minor, and his central message, like that of James, echoes the teaching of Jesus, telling his readers to treat each other with love and sympathy and with generosity and courtesy. They should never return insult for insult. Their calling is to do good, and they need to be able to face God with a clear conscience. It is entirely in accordance with the teaching of Jesus that Peter stresses the importance of humility and asserts that God is against pride. But he also tells them, in phrases which quote the Old Testament, that all of them, not just a select few, are "a chosen generation, a royal priesthood, an holy nation, a peculiar people", unified in Christ and in love, and seeking to spread this loving communion to all mankind and throughout time.

He tells his readers to keep clear of their lower natures and live in a way which is an example to those around them. As with Paul, it is worth recognizing that he is writing as a first-century Jewish man, not as the mouthpiece of God, and when he tells them that they should obey man-made authority, such as the representatives of the emperor, and that servants should submit to their masters and bear unjust punishment patiently, he is concerned that Christians should not get a bad name by behaving in a manner which flouts the customs of the time. As it happens, he is also echoing the advice of Jesus that one should give to Caesar what is Caesar's and to God what is God's. As with Paul, one needs to be aware of the circumstances in which he was writing.

While on the one hand he tells wives to obey their husbands, on the other he says that every husband should seek to understand his wife and see her as an equal heir of the grace of eternal life. Such writings should be understood in the context of the customs and attitudes of the time in which they were written. They should not be taken out of context to support prejudices, such as a predilection for male dominance. The apostles had no more intention than Jesus to abolish slavery or establish equality for women. But they were at the beginning of a movement and an attitude of mind which would eventually lead to such changes.

Peter believed that they were living near the end of things, and that being so, it was all the more important that Christians should love one another and behave in a manner which reflected that. They should be hospitable and should use whatever talents they had to serve others. Like Jesus he could use pictorial language, and he warns his readers that their enemy, the devil, is always about, prowling like a lion roaring for its prey. They must resist him and stand firm in the faith.

There is a problem with what is known as the second letter of Peter, because much of it appears to have been written long after his death, and also because parts of it, such as its warnings against false teachers, has little to do with the teaching of Jesus. But whoever wrote it, it is worth noticing that the message near the beginning is still that a man's faith must bear fruit in a good life.

The other apostle whose views we can see from his letters is John, and again it is the same message, but with a different emphasis. In this case the emphasis is on the importance of love. There is a story told about John that, when he was a very old man and the last survivor of those who had known Jesus intimately, he was often asked to speak to groups of Christians.

He would get up and say, "My brothers and sisters, just love one another. That is all". Then he would sit down again. There is no way of knowing if that ever really happened. But that does not matter. The fact that the story was told about John tells us something. In the first of his surviving letters, he reminds his readers how important it is to love one another and stresses that love is not just a matter of words. If it is genuine, it will show itself in actions.

John tells us that the way to know the Father is to know the Son. He sees the Son as the Way, the Truth and the Light by which men come to God. We know, he says, that God is good, and similarly we know that a man who lives a good life is a true child of God. Everything depends on love, and that means love for one's fellows as well as for God. A man who claims to love God but hates his brother is, says John, a liar. "If he does not love his brother whom he has seen, he cannot love God, whom he has not seen". John also tells his readers that any man who claims to know God but does not obey his laws is both a liar and deluded. It is by obeying God's laws that a man can express his love of God. The test of whether or not a man is living in a right relationship with God is whether or not he obeys his commands.

Each of these four has a different emphasis. Paul's is on the priority of faith over the Law: "The Law killeth but the Spirit gives Life". James's is on the importance of good behaviour, which is the fruit of faith: "Faith without works is dead". Peter's is on the nature of the Christian community, "a chosen generation, a royal priesthood, an holy nation, a peculiar people". John's is on love: "God is love; he who dwells in love is dwelling in God, and God in him".

All four are united in the belief that Christians must love the Being they think of as God, and must love their fellow human beings as well. Similarly, they are united in the belief that it is important to trust in the teaching and example of Jesus rather than be concerned with meticulous obedience to the Law. They agree that love of God and one's neighbour and trust in the teaching and example of Jesus will result in living a good life and doing good works. Finally, they agree that that message is one worth spreading throughout the world. They are propagating ideas which they had learnt from Jesus. If his message was in any way distorted, it was only in that each of them emphasized a particular aspect of his teaching.

Chapter 3

The Early Fathers of the Church

The teaching of Jesus was largely about how people should behave and how they should look at things. Paul went on from that to argue that no one gets into a right relationship with God by meticulous obedience to the Law. Of course, any human society needs laws, and usually they should be obeyed, but to live well it is more important to have faith, or trust, in the teaching and example of Jesus. James wrote of the importance of faith issuing in good works, Peter of the nature of a Christian community, and John of the overriding importance of love.

A quite separate issue which is important to many Christians, both past and present, is the nature of the relationship between Jesus and God the Father, and that is first touched on in a letter written about sixty years after Jesus's ministry, either by Paul himself or possibly by Timothy, to the Christians at Colossae, a town in Asia Minor about a hundred miles inland from Ephesus. After the first few hundred introductory words of greeting and reassurance they were told that "Christ is the visible expression of the invisible God. He existed before creation began, for it was through Him that everything was made, whether spiritual or material, seen or unseen". In its time of writing, though not in its position in the Bible, it is the earliest suggestion of something divine about Jesus.

It is followed, possibly some thirty or more years later, by the far better known passage at the beginning of John's gospel in which he says that at the beginning of time there already existed something which he calls the *logos*, "the Word", and he goes on to say that "the Word became flesh; he came to dwell among us, and we saw his glory, such glory as befits God's only Son, full of grace and truth".

For some hundreds of years Greek philosophers (and "philosophy" is simply a word which means the love of wisdom – or wanting to understand things better) had been trying to understand the origin of life. *Logos*, which literally means simply "word", was used metaphorically for that universal, or divine, wisdom, which they saw as the origin of all things. So educated second-century Greeks would have understood perfectly well what John was getting at when he began like this. The translation, or paraphrase, which follows may not be very elegant and certainly lacks the beauty of the translation in the Authorized, or King James, Version of the Bible, but I hope it makes clear what John was asserting:

At the beginning of time all that existed was divine wisdom, and that divine wisdom is an essential aspect of what we mean by "God". It existed as part of God from the beginning. It was the means whereby all creation took place, and nothing was ever created other than through or by means of this "divine wisdom". The creative, or life, force was in it, and that life force shone like a light in the darkness of primeval chaos, and the darkness has never been able to put it out.

Where John will have surprised some of his readers is by going on to identify the *logos*, the source of all creation, with Jesus. The passage ends with the assertion that "the Word was made flesh and dwelt among us (and we beheld his glory, the glory as of the only begotten of the Father) full of grace and truth".

They would not have been quite so much surprised if they had already come across the idea expressed in the earlier letter to the Colossians, that "Christ is the visible expression of the invisible God". What John is proclaiming at the beginning of his gospel is what Paul had already taught: that the man Jesus was also divine wisdom in human form. In the 252 words of the prologue to his gospel, John sets out what became the essence of

Christian teaching about how the eternal Word (the *logos*) took human form as a manifestation of God on Earth, and became the man Jesus, who was also divine. It is an idea which was going to exercise the minds of the next generation of Christian thinkers.

Towards the end of John's gospel, in the fourteenth chapter, there is a passage in which Jesus tells his close followers that he will be leaving them and adds, "You know where I am going and you know the road I am going to take". Thomas replies, "Lord, we don't know where you are going, and how can we know the way you are going to take?" To that we are told that Jesus answered, "I am the Way and the Truth and the Life. No one comes to the Father except through me", and later, in reply to Philip, he said, "The man who has seen me has seen the Father".

Those comments are explanations to his closest followers that the way to behave, the way to come to God or to His spiritual kingdom, is not by conscientious obedience to the Law but rather by simply following his own example and teaching. In the language of our own time, the answer to the question of what one should do in response to a difficult problem is not to consider principles, such as Justice, Liberty and Equality, for example, which can be seen as modern equivalents of the Law, but rather to ask oneself what Jesus would have done in those circumstances. We won't always give ourselves the right answer, but it is usually a better way of solving problems than appealing to principles. Appeal to any principle can usually be answered by appeal to some other principle.

That passage raises the question of just what was the nature of the relationship of Jesus to the Father, and immediately after it, John puts into Jesus's mouth a long, extended prayer about relationships: his own relationship with the Father, his relationship with his disciples, their relationship with the Father, and their relationships with each other. He also speaks about "the Spirit of Truth, who comes from the Father and whom I will send to you from the Father", and that in turn has produced speculation on the relationship between the Father, the Son and the Holy Spirit.

By now we have moved a long way from Jesus's teaching about how we should behave, how we should look at things, and how we should ensure that we are in a right relationship with God and with our neighbours. We have moved a long way from Paul's principal message that what matters is trust in the teaching and example of Jesus, whom he proclaims as Lord and Saviour, the Messiah, or Christ, the anointed one of Israel. Christian thinking and teaching was already at this very early stage considering what should be believed about the nature of Jesus, his relationship with the Father, and besides that his relationship with the Holy Spirit.

As the Gospel, or Good News, spread through the Graeco-Roman world, it became increasingly necessary to explain Christian ideas and justify them to converts and potential converts, to officials of the Roman Empire, to Jews and those who lived in the countryside, the *pagani*, or pagans, as well as to town-dwellers. It was a task technically known later as apologetics. Sometimes it was a relatively simple matter of seeking to explain how Christians were expected to see things and behave.

One particularly attractive example of explaining the Christian way of life is the anonymous *Letter to Diognetus* of the mid-second century, in which the unknown author was very probably writing to the philosopher Diognetus who had been tutor to Marcus Aurelius, later the Roman emperor from 161 until 180. In that letter the author describes how, wherever they live, Christians follow the customs of that country "in dress, food and general manner of life", but are aware of a higher calling. "They pass their life on earth, but they are citizens of heaven. They obey the established laws, but they outdo the laws in their own lives".

It is clear that there was no requirement on Christians to dress in any particular way or wear any particular badge or other symbol of their religion, but they were expected to obey the laws of whatever society they were living in, and they were expected to have higher standards of behaviour than those required by that law. Understandably, the author also asks if it is right that people who live by the principle of loving everyone should be persecuted.

At about the same time as that letter was being written to Diognetus, i.e. in the middle of the second century AD, another Christian writer, Justin Martyr (the name by which he is known proclaims how his life ended), was trying to persuade the Roman emperor Antoninus Pius, who ruled before Marcus Aurelius, from 138 until 161, of the virtues of the Christian faith. One point Justin made was that vast numbers of people who had lived in the past could be seen as, in a sense, "anonymous Christians". "One article of our faith", he wrote, "is that Christ is the first-begotten of God, and we have already proved him to be the very *logos*, or universal reason, of which mankind are all partakers; and therefore those who live by reason are in some sort Christians, notwithstanding they may pass with you for atheists. Such among the Greeks were Socrates and Heraclitus". By that reasoning Abraham and Moses, for example, and the prophet Isaiah, could also perhaps be seen as, in a sense, pre-Christian Christians.

Justin developed what is called the *logos* theology a step further than did the opening of John's gospel. He taught that while the *logos* was divine, it was distinct from the Father, and at the same time, although it was personal, it was wider than Jesus. On the one hand he taught that Jesus was to be identified with the *logos*, which was divine reason and had existed with the Father before creation. But he also taught that the *logos* had been given expression in the words of the prophets and the teaching of the best Greek philosophers before eventually becoming incarnate in the person of Jesus of Nazareth. That view of things seems to have been well established by the middle of the second century, since it clearly pre-dates his martyrdom in AD 165.

Justin saw Christ's incarnation as the supreme example of God immanent as distinct from God transcendent. Father and Son, he argued, are the same God, but the supreme, unknowable, transcendent God makes contact with the created order through the *logos*, the Word, which is divine reason. Jesus is a light shining in darkness. In his person as God the Son he is separate from God the Father, but only as one torch lit from another is separate; they both shine with the same light. They are two persons of one God. Jesus is a light lit from, and the same as, the one true light: light of light, true God of true God, of one substance with the Father. That is, the underlying reality, or "substance", of Jesus was the same as the underlying reality of the Father.

This view is, of course, metaphorical, intended to illuminate the issue rather than provide a definition, and it is the beginning of systematic theology. But it was not yet fully worked out. Justin was speculating, and in the second century after the birth of Christ he was not alone in speculating about such matters. It was a time rich in speculation, with independence of thought, varied ideas and an instinctive tolerance of and interest in the ideas of others.

But at the same time there was already the problem that some among the leaders of the church wanted certainty and that was accompanied by the danger that the teaching of Jesus, with its provocative and illuminating stories, often throwing questions back to the questioner, would be overtaken by the ideas of those who wanted certainty rather than speculation, with conformity of thought and with any independent thinking suppressed. The idea of heresy, of clinging to a belief contrary to the established teachings of the church, developed hand in hand with this yearning for certainty and for being right about things. Tragically, it resulted in the condemnation of anyone who thought differently.

Justin had written that "after God we worship and love the *logos*, who comes to us from the unbegotten and ineffable God". "Ineffable" means "something too great or intense or sacred to be put into words", and as Justin struggled to get to grips with that problem, he spoke of the *logos* as "another God", which would later be seen as theologically unacceptable and heretical. He also spoke of Jesus as "the begotten God", which was probably more acceptable, but there was clearly a danger that Christianity, which should have been a great liberating force, was already becoming oppressive. At least, when Justin was executed, it was by the Roman authorities, for refusing to sacrifice to the gods, rather than by his fellow Christians.

Another Christian thinker of the first half of the second century whose views were to be influential for most of the next two hundred years, was a man called Marcion, who was the son of a bishop, as leaders of Christian communities were now known. Marcion argued that, because Christianity was a religion of love, there was no place in it for the Hebrew Law. The God of the Hebrew scriptures was a creator who, after creating the world, demanded strict adherence to the Law he had prescribed. The entirely different God described in the gospel of Luke and the letters of Paul was a God of Love, and the purpose of Jesus, the Christ, was to redeem mankind, get rid of the God of the Hebrew scriptures and usher in the entirely new Kingdom of Heaven, in which the grace of the newly revealed Christian God dominates everything and Love has replaced the Law.

That view was not accepted by the leaders of the church. After all, much of the teaching of Jesus was rooted in the Hebrew scriptures, and some of it is only intelligible if one knows the background to it. But Marcion persisted and eventually was excommunicated in 144. That did not stop him spreading his version of Christianity, and it lasted nearly two hundred years, until the Emperor Constantine the Great, despite having issued a decree of toleration, banned a number of dissident or non-conforming groups from meeting, including what were left of the followers of Marcion.

One consequence of the attempt by Marcion to have just Luke's gospel and ten of Paul's letters accepted as the Christian scriptures was that leaders of the Church began to pay attention to the issue of which writings should be accepted. There was widespread agreement that they should include the whole of the Hebrew scriptures, a number of letters written by Paul and other apostles, all three of the synoptic gospels, that is the gospels of Matthew, Mark and Luke, each of which gives a synopsis of the ministry of Jesus, and also Luke's account of the Acts of the Apostles. John's gospel and the Revelation of St John the Divine were accepted later. It was not until the middle of the fourth century that there was general agreement about just which books should be included. Once that agreement was reached, the books which made up what came to be called the New Testament were combined with the Old Testament to form the Holy Bible, which soon came to be seen by most Christians as inspired by God and therefore authoritative.

How and why the letters survived is not clear, but one possibility is that we owe it to a Bishop Onesimus of Ephesus in the early second century. It is possible that he is the same person as the Onesimus who is the subject of Paul's letter to Philemon. After all, Onesimus is not a common name. That letter is the shortest and arguably the most attractive of all Paul's letters, written when Paul was an old man and in prison in Rome, sending a runaway slave, Onesimus, back to his owner, Paul's much-loved friend, Philemon. Paul explains that Onesimus "is already especially loved by me", and he asks Philemon to welcome him back, "not merely as a slave, but as a brother-Christian".

It is a somewhat neglected letter, perhaps partly because people in the twenty-first century find it difficult to adjust their minds to a time when the apostle to the Gentiles would think it appropriate to send a runaway slave back to his owner, even with an assurance that now he will be able to love him. However that may be, it is possible that Bishop Onesimus of Ephesus was that former runaway slave, that he may have saved his own copy of the letter to Philemon and that he may also have gathered together other surviving letters by Paul and a few by other apostles.

At first the church flourished mainly in the eastern Mediterranean, but already in the second century it was spreading westwards through the empire, and one of the earliest Christian theologians in the west was the Greek Bishop Irenaeus of Lyon in Gaul, who was born thirty years after Justin Martyr, in AD 130. Irenaeus argued that the bishops should agree on the teaching of the apostles as recorded in scripture and pass that teaching on to all mankind. "Where the Church is", he wrote, "there is the spirit of God, and where the Spirit of God is, there is the Church and all grace".

The ideal, as Irenaeus saw it, was that bishops should act as spokesmen of a message taught by the apostles and recorded in scripture. That should form the basis for harmony among Christian thinkers and their teaching should not go beyond that. Thus he never ventured into the question which was exercising some minds at the time, of how divinity and humanity could be united in the Son, for we could, he believed, leave to God "mysteries too great for us". It was a wise view which, especially in the light of subsequent bitter controversies among Christians, can be appreciated two millennia later.

Irenaeus rejected vigorously the ideas of Marcion, most particularly because of Marcion's argument that the God of the Old Testament and the God of the New were two separate beings. He insisted that there was just one God, who had created the world, and then, after the disobedience of Adam and the Fall, found a way to redeem mankind through the life and death upon the cross of Jesus. He also, speaking metaphorically, compared the Son and the Holy Spirit to the two hands of God, and so, even without realising it, was unintentionally venturing into the area of theological thinking which was to produce the doctrine of the trinity.

One flourishing part of the Roman Empire in the west was North Africa, where the desert had not yet spread as far north as it has in recent centuries, and there the common language was Latin. But not only had all the books and letters of the New Testament been written in Greek; Justin Martyr, Marcion and Bishop Irenaeus had also all written in Greek. Now Christian doctrine needed to be explained in Latin, taking account of the cultural, social and political circumstances of the west.

Tertullian, a layman writing at the end of the second century in Carthage, whose remains are in modern Tunisia, was born in AD 162, thirty years after Irenaeus and sixty after Justin Martyr, and died in AD 220. He protested at the extent to which Christian theology had been moulded by Greek culture and thinking, and was the first person to write about these matters in Latin. "What has Athens to do with Jerusalem, the Academy with the Church?" he famously asked. Athens was the seat of the Academy, which was the school of philosophy founded by Aristotle. "Why", asked Tertullian, "do we need curiosity when we have Jesus Christ?", and it remained characteristic of Christian thinking in the west that most of it was less philosophical, and at the same time more scriptural, than Christian thinking in the east.

Tertullian was writing at a time when there was still not yet general agreement on either orthodox Christian doctrine or Christian practices, so speculation on both of those aspects of Christianity would continue, not least by Tertullian himself. One element in his teaching which would appeal to modern

Baptists was his belief that the developing practice of baptising small children was mistaken. He insisted on the importance of baptising converted adults and wrote that baptism was "the abolition of sins, which faith secures when sealed in the Father and the Son and the Holy Spirit".

When he wrote that he was clearly thinking in terms of the Holy Trinity, and it was while arguing against Marcion's view that the God of the Old Testament and the God of the New Testament were two different gods, the former a creator and the latter a redeemer, that Tertullian invented the Latin word *trinitas* to describe the relationship between Father, Son and Holy Spirit.

Despite his protests about the pervasive influence of Greek culture, his thinking was strongly influenced by Greek philosophy. He accepted Aristotle's distinction between the "substance" of a thing (its inner, underlying, or "real", being) and its "accidents" (or physical characteristics), and in the light of that he described the trinity as "three persons in one substance" and Christ as "two substances in one person". It was a particularly ingenious and clever way of expressing both the relationship between the three persons of the trinity and the nature of Christ as both God and Man, and its influence was lasting.

But that view of things, distinguishing between the "substance" and the "accidents" of anything, depended on the view of reality developed by Plato and Aristotle which dominated philosophical thinking for about two thousand years, from four hundred years before Christ until at least the fourteenth century. Plato, following up questions which Socrates had asked, had come to the conclusion that there must be a world of *ideas* or *forms*, a "real" world, beyond the world which we perceive with our senses. Underlying every material thing, he argued, is its immutable and eternal *idea* or *form*. Bread, thought Plato, is only bread, and a horse is only a horse, insofar as they approximate to the eternal and unchanging *ideas*, or *forms*, of bread and horse.

Aristotle took this idea of a real world of *ideas* or *forms* a stage further. He decided that the *idea* of anything was its underlying reality. Any material thing will have various external characteristics, or "accidents", such as its texture and shape and how it sounds when struck. But its underlying reality, what makes it what it is, is its "substance". That view of things is known to philosophers as Realism, and it continued to dominate philosophical and theological thinking for more than a thousand years after the time of Tertullian.

The alternative view, which most people who think about these things accept today, is that anything, a loaf of bread or a horse, for example, is simply what it is, and it so happens that we call them "bread" and "horse". That view of things is known to philosophers and theologians as Nominalism. But it was many hundreds of years before any philosophers or theologians began to think that way. Tertullian, for all his scorn of the Academy, was thinking as a Realist, which means that anyone today who is a Nominalist and is interested in the doctrine of the trinity would do well to question the intellectual basis on which Tertullian's thinking rests.

Another of the great early Christian thinkers was Origen, who was born in AD 182, twenty years after Tertullian, and wrote in the east in the first half of the third century. He believed that the purpose of the scriptures was to raise Man from the world of the senses to the world of the spirit and convey eternal truth. It was the spiritual point of a story, not the factual content, which mattered. What is illustrated in the story in John's gospel about Jesus turning water into wine, for example, is that he had, and still has, the power to transform people's lives. Whether or not it is factually true was to Origen relatively unimportant, and he applied this view of things even to the account of Jesus's resurrection.

But where Origen fell out with the church authorities was over his thinking about the relationship between the Father and the Son. He emphasised the separate reality of each of them and tried to solve the problems that arise from that by stressing the identity of the incarnate Christ with the pre-existent *logos*. In the light of Paul's view of Jesus as "the visible expression of the invisible God", together with the *logos* theology in the opening words of John's gospel, that may seem entirely orthodox. But by the time Origen was writing, at the beginning of the third century, anyone who wrote about these issues was liable to be seen as a heretic, holding a personal opinion contrary to the accepted teaching of the church, and that was all the more a problem because on many matters, including how to express the relationship between Jesus and God the Father, the teaching of the church was far from clear.

One person might stress the identity of God the Father with God the Son, thus tending to deny the manhood of Jesus. Another might emphasise their separateness, thus leading either to a denial of the divinity of Jesus or to a belief in two separate gods. And, of course, the problem with all of this is that it owes more to Greek philosophy than to the visual imagery which Jesus so often used to aid understanding. It is a problem which went on causing difficulties down the centuries and continues to do so.

Origen's view was that the Father and the Son were distinct realities or, in Greek, *hypostases*. That provoked strong opposition – so much so that the Bishop of Alexandria objected when Origen was ordained as a presbyter by the bishop of Caesarea, and Origen had to leave Alexandria. He was seen as treating Father, Son and Holy Spirit as separate beings, or even separate gods, and, however much the opening of John's gospel identifies Jesus with the *logos*, which existed with God before the beginning of things, Origen's talk of the pre-existent *logos* was seen by many as being too clever by half.

His views contributed to a developing division between East and West. In the more intellectual east, the western view of the Trinity came to look both naive and barbaric. It looked as if theologians writing in Latin were asserting that the different persons of the trinity were three separate gods. The problem, of course, was a linguistic one. Latin does not contain the range of subtly different words which were available to anyone writing in Greek. But whether writing in Greek or Latin, an attempt was being made to describe the indescribable with words, and no words, even in Greek, are adequate to define the undefinable.

Origen, of course, was using language not so much to define as to give an impression. Thus he spoke of the relationship of the Father to the Son as being like the relationship of the sun to sunshine, and he spoke of the incarnate Christ as being in a sense like a statue depicting the Father. Origen may not be right about everything, but much of his thought is very attractive. For example, in an age when hell was generally thought of as a place under the ground, he saw it as psychological disintegration. He also pointed out that it does not make sense to pray for the cool of spring in the heat of summer. He appreciated that it is not our job to tell God what to do, but rather that the purpose of prayer is that we should become more as we believe God would wish us to be.

What is more, just as Tertullian's thoughts on baptism may appeal to modern Baptists, Origen's ideas about the end of all things will appeal to modern Methodists. He believed that it was God's purpose that at the end of all things all imperfections would be healed and all would be saved. In our spiritual bodies after death all will, in a sense, become divine. Sadly, it was for that that he and his thinking were condemned by the church authorities.

Chapter 4

The Seven Ecumenical Councils in the East

The Christian Church spread through the Roman Empire in the three centuries after the time of Jesus's ministry. It suffered intermittent persecution, but grew as its attractive message about forgiveness of sins, reconciliation and love for God and one's neighbour, appealed to more and more people. No persecution seemed able to prevent its expansion. "The blood of the martyrs is the seed of the church", wrote Tertullian. The way Christians responded to persecution was impressive, and each bout of persecution was followed by further growth.

Inevitably the church differed from one place to another and developed different traditions. The Christian community in Antioch, for example, which is at the north-eastern corner of the Mediterranean, about three hundred miles north of Jerusalem, in what is now the southernmost part of Turkey, developed a tradition which was well established by the end of the second century that it was important to see Jesus as "a man like us, although in every way greater". To emphasise what was divine about him, it was thought, could come dangerously near to suggesting that he was really God masquerading as a man, in the way in which Zeus had been thought to come to Earth in disguise, whether as a man or a bull or a swan. It was important to avoid any suggestion that Jesus was not "a man like us".

Elsewhere, in Alexandria, for example, that Antiochene view was criticised not for being wrong but for its failure to emphasise at the same time that Jesus was also the *logos*, or Divine Wisdom, which had existed from the beginning of all things, thus making him divine as well as human. Throughout the third century Christians speculated about Jesus's nature, about the nature of his relationship with God the Father, and eventually about the nature of their relationship with the Holy Spirit. At that time it was not a cause of disruption, and a wide range of opinions developed.

What men were speculating about was what came to be called the doctrine of the trinity, and at this point I should warn the reader that everything I write about this is liable to be seen by someone as heretical. Because of the controversies within the church over how to write about and define the nature of the trinity, it has become difficult to say anything about it without straying into heresy. Essentially, the accepted view of the church is that God is One, but that that One is also Three, and you can stray into heresy by stressing the Three, thus becoming guilty of Tri-theism, or by treating the Three as different modes of the same One, thus becoming guilty of Modalism.

Within these two broad categories there are any number of different permutations, and it has become so complicated, as one council after another and one theologian after another has attempted to define the indefinable, that there is a standing joke within the Church of England that in most parish churches on Trinity Sunday you will find that the preacher is the newly appointed curate, who has recently left theological college and therefore may just possibly have some idea of what he is talking about.

The idea of the trinity is in a way quite simple. Many people, Jews and Muslims, for example, as well as Christians, worship a Being who is seen as existing beyond us – in heaven. That is particularly well put in a hymn by the Revd Dr Walter Chalmers Smith, who towards the end of the nineteenth century was the Moderator of the Free Church of Scotland. It begins, "Immortal, invisible, God only wise, In light inaccessible hid from our eyes..." In terms of the doctrine of the trinity that is God the Father. But Christians also worship the Son, their Lord and Saviour, Jesus Christ, who is known to them above all through the gospels and is more accessible than God the Father. While the Father is transcendent, existing beyond everything created, the Son is immanent, far more accessible to us, particularly through the gospels. Besides that, many, perhaps most, people also acknowledge something which may be called "conscience" or a "still, small voice of calm", which seems to guide them towards Truth or at least towards a better way of living. That can be described as God the Holy Spirit.

Those three persons, the transcendent God the Father, the immanent God the Son, and the Holy Spirit within us, especially when seen as being in a loving interrelationship with each other, form the God whom Christians worship. It can be something both wonderful and simple. Pope Francis, shortly after his election in 2013, went into a school classroom in Rome and, in response to a child who asked him about the doctrine of the trinity, replied, "The Father made you, the Son saved you, and the Holy Spirit loves you".

The two ideas, that God is One and that God is Three, are, of course, mutually contradictory. Although it is perfectly possible to live with that contradiction, many early Christians felt a need to resolve it. In the first place, they lived in a world in which it seemed important to stress that they worshipped the one and only true God – and that all the other multifarious gods which appeared to be available simply did not exist. But at the same time they acknowledged Jesus as their Lord and Saviour, the Christ, the anointed one, and they were aware of the power of the *pneumatos agiou*, the Holy Spirit. Seeking to find a generally acceptable way of expressing the relationship between Father, Son and Holy Spirit was what gave rise to the doctrine of the trinity.

The last serious period of persecution within the Roman Empire began in AD 303 while Diocletian was emperor and about half a century after the death of Origen, but it only lasted ten years. Then in AD 313, the Emperor Constantine, who was by then ruling in the west, agreed with his colleague who was ruling in the east on a policy of religious freedom throughout the empire, and that policy continued, at least in theory, throughout Constantine's reign, which lasted until 327, by which time he was ruling the whole Roman Empire. He did not seek to make Christianity the only religion of the empire, but he favoured it, and in 324, as he looked for a religion or ideology which would unite rather than divide his empire, he decided to travel to the east and be baptised in the Jordan.

When he arrived, he found that the churches in the east were bitterly divided about the teaching of an Alexandrian presbyter, or priest, called Arius, who had a large popular following but had been excommunicated by his bishop because he asserted that it did not make sense to claim that Jesus, the incarnate Son of God, could be one with the pre-existent *logos*, the Word, that divine or ultimate wisdom which was the first cause of creation. Arius would have been better off in Antioch. In Alexandria, it had got him into serious trouble.

Constantine delayed his baptism and in the following year, 325, summoned a general council of the church to Nicaea on the coast of Asia Minor in order to settle the issue and deal with a whole range of other problems. The emperor took the view that Christians ought to be able to agree on what they should believe, and at the opening of the conference he urged the bishops to seek unity and peace. They did, and all except two of the 220 bishops present (though only half a dozen from the Latin West attended) agreed on a creed, or statement of faith, to be used at baptisms. It reveals clearly the general view among leaders of the Church about what, at the time, they thought to be important.

There was a brief mention of *God, the Father Almighty, Maker of all things, visible and invisible,* and an even briefer mention of *the Holy Spirit.* In between there was a detailed explanation of how Jesus Christ was *of one substance with the Father,* and how it was *by him that all things were made both in heaven and on earth.* Finally, there were detailed condemnations of various unacceptable opinions, such as that *there was a time when he was not.*

All attempts to pin down what Christians should be expected to believe, all creeds, for example, are always and necessarily created in a particular historical context and in response to a particular need. Any statement of belief and any creed can be no more than the best that an individual or a group of Christian thinkers could manage at some particular time when dealing with some particular problem. In this case it is clear that those who drew up the creed felt that they could afford to deal with God the Father and the Holy Ghost briefly, if not perfunctorily, while beliefs relating to Jesus needed to be spelt out in detail.

But the formula agreed at the Council of Nicaea did not settle the issue of how to express the relationship between the Father and the Son. Controversy continued, with theological issues and linguistic problems getting inextricably intermingled with issues of ecclesiastical authority and imperial politics. The issue which was most bitterly fought out during the fourth century was whether the Son was *homoousion toi patri* ("of the same substance as the Father") or *homoiousion toi patri* ("of a similar substance to the Father"). The word *homo* in Greek meant "the same", while the word *homoi* meant "similar". There was just one Greek letter different (the letter i, or iota) and wars were fought over that difference.

The most vociferous advocate in the fourth century of the view that Jesus was "of the same substance as the Father" was Athanasius of Alexandria. Elected to the patriarchate of Alexandria in 328, while still a young man in his early thirties, his views were so different from those of most of his colleagues in the east that he was excommunicated and fled to the west. Restored as Patriarch of Alexandria in 346, he was driven out by military force ten years later and died in 374, five years before his view triumphed at the Council of Constantinople in 381.

Meanwhile, from about the middle of the century and for the next thirty years three theologians, known to history as the Cappadocian Fathers, all living in what is now Turkey, were thinking, writing and exchanging ideas about the three persons of the Holy Trinity and about the relationship between them. Basil, Bishop of Caesarea, his younger brother, Gregory, Bishop of Nyssa, and their friend, Gregory of Nazianzus, who was briefly Patriarch of Constantinople, were all about the age of fifty in 381, when the Emperor Theodosius called the Council of Constantinople, the second of the seven great ecumenical councils, and their ideas had an influence on the final wording of the creed produced at that council, and which is known as the Nicene Creed because it was based on what had been discussed at Nicaea back in 325.

In this time of continuing disagreement about the relationship between the persons of the trinity, the Cappadocian Fathers tried hard to avoid emphasising the unity of the divine nature so much as to deny the separate natures of the three persons of the trinity, and at the same time they tried to avoid emphasising those separate natures so much as to suggest that there were three separate gods. One important element in Basil's thinking was his emphasis on the divinity of the Holy Spirit, for that led all three of them to speculate about the interrelationship of the three persons of the trinity: Father, Son and Holy Spirit.

What is particularly striking and helpful about their approach is that they concentrated not so much on finding an acceptable definition as on understanding the ways in which Father, Son and Holy Spirit are experienced. The transcendent Father is in large measure beyond our comprehension, and they realised that we cannot describe the incomprehensible with words. Even to use the word "He" throws up the problem that it implies that "the Father" is a person, when necessarily "He" (or "She" or "It") is beyond personality.

While they saw the Father as transcendent, they saw the Son as immanent. As the *logos*, or divine wisdom, he was, they taught, involved with the Father (and, indeed, the Holy Spirit) in the act of creation, but as the Word made flesh, he was a man, and truly a man – not God pretending to be a man. At the same time the Holy Spirit is within us and can be experienced directly as our conscience or as a guiding light.

The Cappadocian Fathers also stressed the unique position of the Father as the source of divinity. The other two persons of the trinity, the Son and the Holy Spirit, both derived from the Father, and the ways in which that was so were expressed by the Cappadocian Fathers in pictorial, or metaphorical, language. Neither was created. Instead, the Son was begotten (or alternatively, the Word was uttered), and while the Father begat the Son, he breathed the Spirit.

That pictorial language is intended to give some understanding of the nature of the relationship between the persons of the trinity. Like so much else in Christianity it should not be taken literally, and indeed, the notion of God the Father begetting the Son in primeval chaos, before the beginning of time and before they were both involved in creation is, if taken literally, either ludicrous or offensive. The important point is that both the Son and the Holy Spirit derive from, or proceed from, that divinity which is God the Father, and they were perceived by the Cappadocian Fathers to co-operate with Him in all aspects of what the Fathers took to be a divine plan, beginning with the work of creation.

This approach is open to the objection that it can seem to overemphasize the differences between the three persons of the trinity and comes dangerously near to setting up three separate but related gods, which is exactly what the objection was to Arianism. To that the Cappadocian Fathers replied that although it is "appropriate" to think of the Father creating, the Son redeeming and the Spirit guiding, all three persons of the trinity are intimately involved in each of those activities. That view of the trinity has had a lasting effect.

In the event, the Council of Constantinople in 381 reaffirmed the creed along the lines agreed at Nicaea back in 325. Above all it confirmed that the Son was *homoousion toi patri*, i.e., of the same substance as the Father – not a similar substance. A new article declared that the Holy Spirit "who with the Father and Son together is worshipped and glorified", proceeds from the Father, and it was now asserted that the Son was "begotten of his Father". That, of course, does not relate to the begetting of the infant Jesus but to the Son, the *logos*, who, it was being asserted, was "begotten of his Father before all worlds". It was a reaffirmation of the *logos* theology, the idea that Jesus should be seen as an incarnation of the Divine Wisdom which had existed before the beginning of time. The begetting of the infant Jesus, when he became "incarnate by the Holy Spirit of the Virgin Mary", was a separate matter. The main change from what had been asserted at Nicaea in 325 was the omission of the anathemas condemning Arianism. That issue was seen to be closed, and the formula now was as follows:

We believe in one God, the Father Almighty, Maker of heaven and earth, and of all things visible and invisible.

And in one Lord Jesus Christ, the Only Begotten Son of God, born of the Father before all ages. God from God, Light from Light, true God from true God, begotten, not made, of the same substance as the Father, by whom all things were made. For us men and for our salvation he came down from heaven, and was incarnate by the Holy Spirit of the Virgin Mary, and became man.

For our sake he was crucified under Pontius Pilate, he suffered death and was buried, and rose again on the third day in accordance with the Scriptures. He ascended into heaven and is seated at the right hand of the Father. He will come again in glory to judge the living and the dead and his kingdom will have no end.

And in the Holy Ghost, the Lord and Giver of life, who proceedeth from the Father, who with the Father and the Son together is worshiped and glorified, who spake by the prophets.

And In one holy catholic and apostolic Church; we acknowledge one baptism for the remission of sins; we look for the resurrection of the dead, and the life of the world to come. Amen.

There was an overwhelming majority in favour of the formula *homoousion toi patri* (of the same substance as the Father), probably because that phrase was sufficiently ambiguous to be interpreted in two different ways. On the one hand it can be seen as asserting a rather general identity, thus leaving plenty of room for distinguishing between the different persons of the Father and the Son. On the other hand, it can be seen as asserting a sufficiently specific identity of Father and Son as to rule out any possibility of seeing them as two separate gods.

Whatever view those attending the council took on this issue, it is clear that they were concerned less with the teaching of Jesus than with how Christians should be expected to think about him. Three hundred years earlier Jesus had proclaimed the Kingdom of Heaven, and had taught his followers to pray that the will of the Father might be done "on Earth as it is in heaven". Now his followers were proclaiming him as the Son of God, with their beliefs about his nature set out in a creed. In the words of the early twentieth century German theologian Rudolf Bultmann, *Der Verkündiger wurde zum Verkündigter*, "the proclaimer became the proclaimed".

Theodosius declared the version of the creed agreed at Constantinople in 381 as the official religion of the empire and required his subjects to give assent to it. Rather strangely it was still known as the Nicene Creed. It makes no mention of the trinity, but it was seen as setting out what came to be thought of as the Trinitarian rather than the Arian view of God. The difference between those two views was never as clear as was later assumed. Nor were they the only options, and much depended on the language being used. But that "Nicene" creed now constituted the orthodoxy (i.e. "correct belief") of the catholic, (i.e., "universal") church, to which Christians within the empire were required to give assent. Free discussion of theological ideas was no longer tolerated. The church became an office of state for religious affairs, and the lay state imposed uniformity.

The Christian church had been established in the empire in three stages. During the first three centuries it spread through its virtues and despite persecution. Through much of the fourth century it flourished and grew under imperial favour and patronage. Then in the last two decades of that century, from the proclamation of the Nicene Creed at the Council of Constantinople in 381 onwards, it was established in power by imperial legislation. Backed by the authority of the emperor it now required conformity of thought and was able to persecute pagans, with the word "pagans" now being used not just for those dwelling in the countryside but for all non-Christians.

It could also persecute its own dissidents, and in 385, just four years after the Council of Constantinople, the church for the first time had some of those it regarded as heretics executed. The victims were Priscillian, the Bishop of Avila in central Spain, together with six of his followers, who were all accused of and condemned for "sorcery". It may be, though this is not certain, that they had been attracted by Dualism, which is sometimes referred to as Manicheism, because it derives from the ideas of Mani, who lived in Mesopotamia in the third century. Accounts of it vary, but most of its adherents seem to have believed that there were two gods (hence Dualism): an evil god who presided over Darkness and had created all material things, and a good god who presided over Light and had created all things spiritual.

Whether or not Priscillian and his followers had become Manichees, the fact remains that it was just three-quarters of a century since the end of the Diocletian persecution, and that now the persecuted had become the persecutors. But one needs to recognise that the Christians who were martyred under Diocletian had not died for freedom of thought or religious toleration, but because they thought they were right. Three-quarters of a century later their successors still thought that they were right, but now they were members of the official church of the empire, and they were able to insist on at least outward conformity to the orthodox teaching of the church.

Theological speculation moved on to more detailed consideration of the nature of Christ. Could he be both God and Man? If he was both, could he be one person? The issue became a public problem soon after a monk from Antioch, Nestorius, became the Patriarch of Constantinople in 428. Nestorius, following the Antiochene tradition, disliked having the term *Theotokos*, God-bearer, applied to Mary, the mother of Jesus, and he caused offence by asserting that "God is not a baby two or three months old". He was entirely happy that she should be venerated as *Christotokos*, or Christbearer, but not that she should be seen as bearing in her womb the God who was the creator of all things.

The patriarch Cyril of Alexandria saw that as dangerously heretical. He, following the Alexandrian tradition associated with Athanasius, wanted to stress the unity of Christ's person as God and Man combined. It was because of this controversy that Theodosius II in 431 summoned the bishops of Christendom to Ephesus for the third ecumenical council. The council began with Cyril of Alexandria excommunicating Nestorius. Then the patriarch of Antioch arrived and deposed Cyril. Next legates from Rome arrived and supported Cyril. Nestorius, who had no wish to engage in public controversy, gave up and asked to return to his monastery, and the declaration which emerged from the council followed Cyril's belief.

The Alexandrian view had prevailed over that associated with Antioch. Jesus was a single and undivided person, who was both God and Man at the same time. To see him simply as an ideal man, whose essential humanity was somehow infused with the divine, was to err into heresy. Mary was *Theotokos*, God-bearer, or Mother of God – a God who had existed from the beginning of all things. That is, she bore in her womb a baby who was the creator of all things and had existed before his incarnation and before time as the Word, the *logos*.

It was a ruling which the many churches which followed the Antiochene tradition could not accept, and it resulted in lasting schism. Most of them were beyond the borders of the Roman Empire, and they were particularly well established in Persia. This Church of the East survived for centuries, cut off from communion with their fellow-Christians in the "catholic" and "orthodox" church of the Roman Empire, because they believed in the essential humanity of Jesus.

The Council of Ephesus appeared to be a triumph for the Alexandrian emphasis on the unity of Christ's person as God and Man combined. But it had not settled the issue. Not only had it resulted in lasting schism with the Church of the East; even within the empire there were many who remained attached to the Antiochene Christology. They could not and would not get away from the point that, even if Jesus was both God and Man, there had to be some difference between his Godhead and his Manhood, or else one would be saying that God and Man are the same thing.

The outcome, in 451, only twenty years after the Council of Ephesus, was yet another council, this time at Chalcedon, just across the Bosphorus from Constantinople. Its task was to find a formula which could accommodate the Antiochene Christological view, with its emphasis on the essential humanity of Jesus, with what was now orthodoxy. The formula which emerged is on the one hand very impressive and very clever, but on the other so complex in its language that the reader may prefer to skip it:

> Jesus Christ was, it proclaimed, *at once complete in Godhead and complete in manhood, truly God and truly man, consisting also of a reasonable soul and body; of one substance (homoousion) with the Father as regards his Godhead, and at the same time of one substance with us as regards his manhood; like us in all respects, apart from sin; as regards his Godhead, begotten of the Father before the ages, but yet as regards his manhood begotten, for us men and for our salvation, of Mary the Virgin, the God-bearer (Theotokos); one and the same Christ, Son, Lord, Only-begotten, recognised in two natures, without confusion, without change, without division, without separation; the distinction of natures being in no way annulled by the union, but rather the characteristics of each nature being preserved and coming together to form one person and subsistence (hypostasis), not as parted or separated into two persons, but one and the same Son and Only-begotten God the Word (logos), Lord Jesus Christ.*

It is an entirely different world from the down to earth language of Jesus's parables, and even this desperate attempt to find some way of agreeing failed. The previous council, at Ephesus in 431, had driven into schism those who emphasised the humanity of Jesus. Now the Council of Chalcedon of 451, the fourth of the ecumenical councils, drove into schism those, largely in Egypt and Syria, who emphasised the essential unity of Jesus's nature, and who were now persecuted as heretics.

The Christian church was triumphant within the Roman Empire, which provided not only peace and prosperity within its bounds but also the light of the gospels. One effect of that was that the bounds of Christendom now appeared to be coterminous with the bounds of the *Pax Romana*. Within the borders of the empire was light. Beyond was darkness. For centuries the leaders of the Christian church did little or nothing to spread the Good News of Christ to the neighbouring Arab world. They were more concerned with the niceties of theology than with following the command of Jesus to "make disciples of all the nations". A second Council of Constantinople, called in 553 by the Emperor Justinian, and a third Council of Constantinople, called in 681 by the Emperor Constantine IV, were further attempts to find an acceptable wording to settle the Christological controversy. Both had only temporary success.

In 628, while the leaders of the Christian church in the eastern part of the empire were still far more concerned with theological niceties than with reaching out to try to convert the pagan Arab peoples, an Arab mystic, Muhammad, rode into Mecca on a camel at the head of 10,000 followers to establish the holiest shrine of the new religion which he had already proclaimed in the town of Medina six years earlier. The religion was Islam, or surrender to God, and its followers were Muslims, people who had surrendered themselves to God.

A few years later the Arabs burst out of their homeland proclaiming the simple and clear message that "there is no God but Allah and Muhammad is his prophet". Within a few years all the land of the patriarchates of Alexandria, Antioch and Jerusalem was in their hands. Many schismatic Christians welcomed the Muslims as liberators and were able to live for some centuries under Islamic rulers, tolerated as they had not been by their fellow Christians. As the seventh century went by the Muslims overran North Africa, cut the Eastern Orthodox Church off from the Western Catholic Church by their control of the Mediterranean, and even besieged Constantinople.

An apparently separate issue which tore the Eastern Church apart in the eighth century was the issue of whether or not it was acceptable to use pictures of the saints, and more particularly of Christ, in worship. These pictures, known as icons, were seen as symbols of that which they represented and consequently were treated with veneration. But there was also a long tradition in the east of opposition to the use of pictures and statues in worship. The second of the commandments given to the Hebrew people by Moses forbad the making of graven images, and Muslims similarly objected to the graphical representation of any living creature and decorated their mosques with geometric patterns.

Within the Christian church the issue was an extension of the Christological controversy. The case against icons was that it is impossible to portray the divine, and since Christ was divine it was impossible to portray him. To attempt to do so was blasphemous. The case in favour of them was that Jesus was human, and to assert that it was wrong to depict him was a denial of his humanity. Roman emperors (in modern times described as Byzantine emperors) pursued an iconoclast policy through much of the eighth century, but the issue was eventually settled in favour of the use of icons at the seventh and last of the ecumenical councils of the church, the Second Council of Nicaea, in 787.

The seven great ecumenical councils had over a period of nearly half a millennium established what the church asserted were the essentials of Christian belief. The First Council of Nicaea of 325 and the First Council of Constantinople of 381 had settled how to express the relationship between the persons of the trinity and had produced the Nicene Creed, which is still used today. All the others were concerned with establishing what Christians should be expected to believe about how far Jesus was human and how far and in what way he was divine.

Ephesus in 431 had the effect of driving into schism those who emphasised his humanity. Chalcedon in 451 drove into schism those who were seen as excessively emphasising the unity of his human and divine natures. The Second and Third Councils of Constantinople, in 553 and 681 respectively, were further attempts at finding a formula which everyone could be required to accept. Even the decision of the Second Council of Nicaea, the seventh and last of the ecumenical councils, to uphold the veneration of icons, was really a decision on the Christological issue, in this case upholding the humanity of Jesus.

It was not an issue which could be dealt with to everyone's satisfaction in words. The tragedy was that everyone involved agreed that Christ was truly human and also in some sense divine, but they could not agree on the words to define it. They were trying to express the inexpressible.

Chapter 5

The West and Augustine of Hippo

Although the Orthodox Church in the eastern Mediterranean neglected to seek to convert the Arab peoples in the South, some Christians did seek to preach the good news of Christ to the barbarian peoples in the north. One of the earliest and most successful of these missionaries was a Visigoth called Ulfilas. His name is an affectionate diminutive meaning "Little Wolf". His father was a Visigoth, but his mother was the daughter of Greeks from Cappadocia who had been taken captive by the Goths. He was born early in the fourth century, came to Constantinople as a young man, and when he was thirty, probably between ten and twenty years after the Council of Nicaea of 325, was consecrated as Bishop of the Goths.

At that time orthodox theology about the nature of the trinity, and in particular the relationship between the Father and the Son, was still not yet settled, and the Christianity which Ulfilas proclaimed successfully to the Goths was closer to Arianism than to what later came to be accepted as orthodoxy. He worked among the Goths for forty years until his death, and was so successful that the Goths in turn provided most of the missionaries who converted the other Germanic tribes which were infiltrating and eventually invading the empire.

Consequently, it was an Arian form of Christianity which characterised the worship of the Visigoths, who established a kingdom in south-west Gaul and in Spain, the Ostrogoths, who came to dominate Italy and much of the Dalmatian coast, and the Vandals, who conquered the western part of North Africa. It was also the form of Christianity accepted by a number of other tribes, such as the Burgundians, the Lombards and the Suevi, but it did not reach the Franks, who established themselves in the north of Gaul and were still pagans until the end of the fifth century.

Most of these barbarians who flooded into the western part of the empire had not come to destroy Rome but to share in what it had to offer. Part of what it offered was Christianity, and if the first version of Christianity they encountered was Arianism, that is what they accepted. Conversion was often a matter of persuading a war-leader, or king, about what to believe, and once the king was persuaded, his whole people, or tribe, would join him in being baptised. One consequence of this was that Arianism, which had begun in the East as an intellectual solution to a difficult theological problem, came eventually to be regarded as the simple-minded view of barbarians in the West. It was vigorously opposed and steps were taken to persuade the barbarians that, if they were to be proper Christians, they had to conform to the Trinitarian teachings of the orthodox and catholic, or "universal", church.

Those teachings were much influenced by an outstanding thinker called Augustine who was born in November 354 to a pagan father and a Christian mother. They lived in a settlement called Thagaste in what is now Algeria but was then in the Roman province of Numidia in North Africa. Apart from five years in his late twenties and early thirties, when he was in Italy, Augustine lived all his life in that area, either in Thagaste or, in his teens, in the Numidian metropolis of Carthage, and then, in the second half of his life, in the seaport of Hippo, which was about forty-five miles from Thagaste. His father had a few acres of land and a few slaves, a wife and three children, and the family were what we would think of as being members of the middle class.

When Augustine was sixteen, his father died. A year later he went to Carthage, where he discovered sex, enjoyed it, and before long, while still a teenager, set up home with a girl of a lower class. The law did not allow him to marry her, but he could, and did, co-habit with her as his concubine, or what we would call a "common law wife". They were soon teen-age parents, with a much-loved son whom they called Adeodatus ("Given by God"), and they lived together, apparently in mutual harmony, for about the next twelve years.

In Carthage Augustine also discovered Dualism and became a member of a Manichean group – not one of the Elect, who were expected to live a life of extreme asceticism, but a Hearer, who could live altogether more self-indulgently. According to his own *Confessions*, published when he was in his forties, he was an enthusiastic member, who thought and wrote and spoke about the merits of Dualist ideas, converting a number of those around him to the teachings of Mani. He remained a Manichee for ten years, and in later life his enemies accused him of never having completely put aside Dualist ideas.

The third thing which Augustine discovered at Carthage was the accumulated literary and philosophical culture of Rome. He was a quite exceptionally clever young man and imbibed not only the philosophical dialogues of Cicero and Seneca but also the ideas of the Greek philosopher Plato in the Latin form available at the time, and late in life he thought of Platonist philosophy as close to Christianity. He began to think seriously about ethical and religious issues, and it was from Cicero that he learnt that the search for power or honour or wealth or sex is not the route to happiness. Later in life he concluded that that applied not only to individuals but to whole societies.

His outstanding ability and the elegance and skill of his writing led to a teaching post in Carthage and then, in 383, to a post in Rome teaching rhetoric, the study of how to write and speak clearly and appropriately. It was at this stage of his life that he began to have doubts about Manicheism. He was also becoming interested in such questions as how we can know anything, how we can be sure about it, and how far words are an effective means of communication, and he was seeking an alternative to Manicheism when, shortly afterwards, in 384, he was appointed, while still not yet thirty, to be the professor of rhetoric at Milan.

Augustine now had the prospect of significant secular advancement, for Milan was then effectively the capital of the empire. It was there that the emperor had his court and headquarters, because it was better situated strategically than either Rome or Constantinople for dealing with the increasing threat from the Goths. But living with a Carthaginian concubine was an obstacle to secular ambition, so his mother arranged for the young woman (we are never told her name) to be sent back to Africa, and then found an heiress of a suitable class for him to marry. His prospective wife was still a couple of years short of puberty, when she would be able to marry, so for the moment Augustine took another concubine. It was not successful. He ended the relationship, and gradually both the idea of a suitable marriage and his ambition fell away.

He was going through a significant change which led eventually to his conversion to catholic Christianity. As the new professor of rhetoric he had met Ambrose, the Bishop of Milan, who had been persuaded ten years earlier to give up his secular post as the governor of the province and accept the leadership of the Christian community there. At that time Ambrose was the most significant figure in the western catholic Church, more important in the affairs of the church than the then pope. He was, like Augustine, a man of considerable intellect. He was also an impressive preacher. Augustine went to hear him preach, and that was one of the factors which led to Augustine's conversion to catholic Christianity.

On becoming a Christian, Augustine put aside both ambition and sex. He now saw himself as chosen by God to lead a new life of celibacy, and, undistracted by sex, he could use his intellect to think and write about God. He was baptised at Easter 387, together with his son, Adeodatus, and in the autumn of 388, at the age of thirty-three, he returned to Africa, where, with a group of friends, he created a small ascetic community. They lived a simple life at Thagaste, with no fixed rule, but as a "society of brothers", away from the cares of the world, thinking about and discussing philosophical and theological issues. Adeodatus had reached an age when he was able to discuss such matters with his father, but within a year of their return to Thagaste he died, still in his teens.

None of the community at Thagaste was a priest, or presbyter, but when, early in 391, Augustine visited the seaport of Hippo, he found that his reputation had gone before him. The bishop welcomed him and told his congregation how much he needed a presbyter to assist him, and Augustine was constrained to accept ordination. He did not want to be a pastor, preferring a life of contemplation and discussion with like-minded friends, but he did not think he could properly refuse.

The bishop allowed him to set up a community which was rather like what was later called a monastery, and then, nearing death, he arranged for Augustine to be consecrated as a bishop with him in order to secure the succession. It was probably from 397 onwards that Augustine was independently carrying out all the duties of a bishop, and for more than thirty years, until his death in 430, he preached to his local congregation, arbitrated in local disputes, administered the sacraments, and dealt with all the affairs of his diocese, while at the same time finding time to produce a mass of theological writings.

He was seventy-five when he died in August 430. He had lived through three-quarters of a century in which the Roman Empire was bit by bit losing its authority in the west and at the same time much about the empire's religion was unsettled. When Augustine was born, back in 354, the then emperor, Constantius II, was one of the sons of Constantine the Great. Augustine was still a child during the brief reign, from 361 to

363, of Julian the Apostate, who tried to return the empire to its traditional pagan religion.

During the five years he was in Italy as a young man, from 383 until 388, the emperor was Theodosius I, who was the first to declare the Trinitarian rather than the Arian form of Christianity as the official religion of the empire. Then, after the death of Theodosius in 395, at about the time that Augustine was consecrated as a bishop while in his early forties, the empire was finally and permanently divided, with one emperor in the east and another in the west.

In 410, by which time Augustine was in his mid-fifties and well-established as Bishop of Hippo, the Goths sacked Rome, and in the summer of 430, as he was dying, the Vandals, who had swept through Gaul and Spain into Africa, were besieging Hippo, which they took shortly afterwards. For nearly the next half century a succession of eleven different emperors struggled on in the west until in 476 the last of them, Romulus Augustulus, was deposed.

Throughout the three and a half decades when he was Bishop of Hippo Augustine thought, wrote and engaged in controversy about theological issues. The first problem he was faced with when he became Bishop of Hippo was that within the city there were two groups of Christians who were bitterly divided. During the Diocletian persecution, which had lasted from 303 for about the next ten years, Christians had not been allowed to worship publicly, so many of them had met privately. Then the authorities had required them to hand over sacred books, so they had perhaps handed over a few heretical books, and when required to hand over church plate, they had found something or other to hand in. Sometimes the authorities had connived at this, if, for example, a Roman governor and the local bishop were friends and both wanted to avoid trouble.

The Donatists, who were particularly strong in the African province of Numidia and took their name from one of their leaders, Donatus, were entirely opposed to any compromise of this sort. The division between the Donatists and the Catholic Christians, who were in communion with Rome, hardened and lasted from one generation to the next. It had continued for about eighty-five years by the time Augustine became Bishop of Hippo, where the Donatists outnumbered the Catholics. The two groups worshipped in their own churches, with the same creed and the same liturgy, but bitterly at enmity.

Augustine made an attempt to achieve reconciliation, but the attempt revealed two fundamental issues on which agreement was impossible. The Donatists had come to believe that the church should be a holy and exclusive community whose members should and could keep themselves pure and do no wrong. Hand in hand with this went the view that the sacraments were only valid if administered by a priest in a state of grace. The sinfulness of a priest administering the sacraments at the Eucharist would invalidate them.

Augustine disagreed with the Donatists on both issues. The first concerned the nature of the church. Augustine's position was that the church was made up of sinners as well as saints. It was up to God to winnow the harvest at the Last Judgement and separate the wheat from the chaff. It was not for Man to judge. On the second issue, concerning the validity of the sacraments, Bishop Stephen of Rome had asserted in the middle of the third century that the validity of the sacraments is independent of any merit or virtue of the minister, and Augustine reaffirmed that.

Disagreement between the Donatists and the Catholics on these two issues made compromise impossible. At first Augustine opposed the idea of the use of force to ensure conformity. He believed that persuasion and reconciliation were preferable. But eventually he came round to the view that force was needed.

If *Amor Dei* (the love of God) did not succeed, *Timor Dei* (the fear of God) might, and so long as the motive for punishing someone was to bring him to repentance, it was always possible that punishment might do more good than further attempts at persuasion. Augustine's view was that the force used should be as little as possible, should under no circumstances include torture or death, and should not be seen as punishment but as a form of loving chastisement aimed at bringing the miscreant back to God.

All the same, it was a dangerous view in a world in which the secular power was issuing edicts against heresy and paganism and could be called upon to enforce conformity of belief – or at least outward conformity. It could be used, and has been used for centuries afterwards, as a justification for taking action against any group which did not conform to the orthodox teachings of the church, and as a justification of the view that it is morally justifiable to use evil means to achieve a just end.

Meanwhile, the main issue dividing the church was the question of how one should see and express the relationship between the persons of the trinity. Augustine saw it as necessary to combat Arianism, which was widely perceived in the west as presenting God as a three-level hierarchy, with the Son subordinate to the Father and the Holy Spirit subordinate to the Son. So he tried to emphasise the essential unity of the Godhead and the equality of the Son with the Father by teaching that the Holy Spirit proceeds from both the Father and the Son. That view was eventually so influential that it became customary in the west to add the extra word *filioque* to the creed, proclaiming that the Holy Spirit proceeded from the Father *and the Son* rather than, as had been agreed in 381 at Constantinople, just from the Father.

The Latin word *filioque* means "and from the Son". The first part, *filio*, means "from the Son" and the last three letters, *"que"*, are a suffix which the Romans added to a word to give the meaning "and". Augustine did not himself insert the *filioque* clause into the creed, but it was his writings which led to it being common practice in the west. This was perceived by the Greeks as introducing a second source of divinity into the Godhead, and was objectionable both on the grounds that it was theologically unsound and also, equally importantly, that it tended towards schism, because the churches of the west were using a different wording in the creed from that agreed by the Council of Constantinople in 381.

Augustine had not intended to contradict what was taught by the Cappadocian Fathers. Still less did he intend to revise the creed agreed at the Council of Constantinople. But his teaching resulted in a very different emphasis in the west, and the insertion of the *filioque* clause into the creed was eventually approved by Pope Benedict VIII in 1014. It has remained for centuries a cause of controversy between the Orthodox churches of the east and the Catholic church in the west, partly because of the issue itself and partly because of the problem that the patriarchs of the east, of Constantinople, Alexandria, Antioch and Jerusalem, all took the view that the Bishop of Rome had overreached his powers by changing a creed agreed in council by the whole church at Constantinople. That problem is still not resolved.

Another consequence of Augustine's teaching about the trinity was that about half a century after his death it resulted in the drawing up, probably in the south of France, of another creed aimed at setting out his teaching. That creed, which is known as the Athanasian Creed, was attributed to Athanasius, who had died some two hundred years earlier, because he was remembered as a staunch opponent of Arianism and an upholder of "orthodoxy" on trinitarian issues, and it begins and ends by declaring that it is a requirement for salvation that it should be believed.

It is a striking example of how far the church had moved from expounding the teaching of Jesus to requiring Christians to conform to official doctrines. It begins with a declaration that anyone wanting to be saved must keep the faith "whole and undefiled" or "without doubt he shall perish everlastingly". It goes on in rather more than six hundred words to try to define the doctrine of the trinity, as taught by Augustine, in sentences such as this: "And in the Trinity none is afore, or after other: none is greater, or less than another; But the whole three persons are co-eternal together: and co-equal. So that in all things, as is aforesaid: the Unity in Trinity and the Trinity in Unity is to be worshipped". It ends with the declaration: "This is the Catholick Faith: which except a man believe faithfully, he cannot be saved". Augustine, who saw himself as struggling to understand better and not as an authority, would, I believe, have been shocked.

While his writings about the nature of the church (i.e., about who forms the Christian community) and about the sacraments (i.e., about when they are and are not valid) were the outcome of his opposition to the Donatists, and his writings about the trinity were the outcome of his opposition to Arianism, his teaching on Grace and on Original Sin arose from combatting Pelagianism. Pelagius, a British monk who had moved to Rome in about the year 400, had been shocked by the moral laxity around him and argued that Christians should behave better and, moreover, that they could if they decided to. God had, after all, made human nature, and in requiring them to be perfect He was only demanding something which He had ensured was possible. In light of the teaching of Jesus, and also in the light of the insistence of the apostle James that faith must lead on to good works, that appears to be reasonable.

The problem for Augustine was that it seemed that Pelagius was teaching that men could save themselves. That is, they could get into a right relationship with God simply by doing good works, and Augustine believed that this denied the importance of the Grace of God. As he saw it, men were corrupted from birth by Original Sin and could not by their own efforts achieve salvation by doing good works. Only the Grace of God could save them. Augustine contrasted the natural sinfulness of mankind with the perfect goodness of God and argued that the salvation of any individual was the consequence of divine intervention. The contrary Pelagian view was condemned by a local synod at Carthage in 418.

Augustine's view of things had a lasting effect on Christian thinking and led both to a denial of free will, and to the view that, if salvation is available only to those elected by God, damnation is the necessary fate of everyone else, an idea much later known as the doctrine of double predestination. In fact, Augustine neither denied free will nor asserted double predestination. He saw the difficulties inherent in the problem he was tackling, and he saw the inadequacy of words to express what he was getting at. He believed that God knows all things, but he also saw God as out of time, as ultimate and eternal Being, rather than something which happens to exist, so God's knowledge was not as ours, with things happening in succession, both in the past and then going on into the future. Thus talk of predestination, as if God had foreseen and predetermined everything which would happen on Earth, did not make sense. But that was too subtle a position to be readily intelligible. Understandably, his critics claimed that he had strayed into matters which God had not revealed and which were beyond human understanding.

Augustine's teaching about the Grace of God is closely associated with his teaching about original sin, which included the view that sin was transmitted from one generation to the next by the sex act, which he saw as intrinsically sinful, with the lustful inclinations of men encouraged by the lasciviousness of women, who tempted them as Eve had tempted Adam. This is a view which is particularly unacceptable in the twenty-first century. But, as usual, Augustine is not completely wrong.

The so-called doctrine of original sin begins to make sense if one thinks of the human condition as one in which human beings are naturally (or originally) self-centred (or sinful). An instinct for self-preservation and a measure of self-centredness were essential for primitive Man to survive, and those who did survive and evolved into what we call human beings did so largely because they had those characteristics. Human beings cannot escape the fact that they always see things from their own position outwards, and in that sense they are naturally self-centred. Jesus knew that and taught his followers that they should throughout life try to escape their natural self-centredness, or original sinfulness, and instead learn to love God and one's neighbour. In that sense, the view that human beings are by nature self-centred, Augustine is right, but not in his view that the sex act was intrinsically sinful because it was the means by which original sin is transmitted.

While much of Augustine's work can best be understood as reactions against Donatism, Arianism and Pelagianism, his greatest work was inspired by the sacking of Rome by the Goths in 410, when he was fifty-six, and by the way the Roman Empire could be seen to be collapsing in the west. He started writing *The City of God* as a meditation on the fall of Rome and completed it thirteen years later, in 427, two years before the Vandal invasion of North Africa and three years before he died, just before the Vandals took Hippo, in 430.

In *The City of God*, he argued that Christians needed to put their trust in the heavenly kingdom – not in the works of Man. "The greatest city in the world has fallen in ruins", he wrote, "but the City of God endureth for ever". He challenged the then widely accepted view that the empire could be seen as the earthly image of the heavenly kingdom. On the contrary, his view of the weakness and corruption of mankind, contrasted with the perfection of God, led him to be very critical of Roman society, in which the rich were very rich, while all around them many were very poor and private almsgiving by the rich did little to solve the problem of poverty.

He quoted Sallust, a Roman historian and politician of the first century BC, who had commented that Roman society was characterised by "private affluence and public squalor", and argued that the problem would only be solved if the state intervened to introduce a system of taxation which redistributed wealth from the rich to the poor. The failings of human society indicated that it was part of a fallen and corrupt world, while the City of God was something divine and entirely different. His thinking about that is clearly in line with the teaching of Jesus, who had insisted that the Kingdom of Heaven was not of this world but rather was a spiritual kingdom.

Augustine thought and wrote a lot, many of his ideas are memorable, and there is much about his writing and his ideas which is attractive. For example, he suggested that, despite Man's fallen nature, because human beings were made "in the image of God" it was natural for them to crave union with God. The way he put that, "You have made us for yourself and our hearts are restless until they rest in you", has resonated with any number of Christians down the centuries. He also argued memorably that an essential qualification for martyrdom is that one should have tried to avoid it.

Some of his thoughts are expressed in aphorisms, such as *Quis cantat bis orat*, "Whoever sings prays twice", and most notably *Dilige et fac quod vis*, "Love and do as you will", which is not a recipe for license but an assertion that love should lead to higher standards of behaviour than will be achieved by scrupulous adherence to rules. One of his aphorisms, "Without God, we cannot. Without us, God will not", sums up his view that no one could live a good life without the help of the Grace of God, while God would not provide that Grace other than to someone who sought it. "God provides the wind. Man must raise the sail", he wrote. It is a view which is a long way from the later over-simplified doctrine of predestination, and even further from the doctrine of double predestination.

Many of Augustine's ideas seem modern. He appreciated the existence of the subconscious mind and realised that it is possible to know something without knowing that you know it. Furthermore, in many of his sermons he warned his congregation that prayer should not be a matter of telling God anything or trying to persuade him to change his mind. Augustine believed that God's will and purpose were unchangeable and that we should therefore use prayer as a way of getting our wills aligned to his. He could also see the danger of people being bitterly disappointed if they engaged in petitionary prayer but did not then get the things they had asked for.

He also understood that biblical writers often used symbolism and allegory, and he saw that insistence on a simple literal meaning of something might mean that one failed to grasp the possibly more important underlying message. He regarded miracles simply as things which we do not understand, for God would never, he believed, act contrary to the laws of nature which he had himself prescribed. He believed that actions are not in themselves good or bad, but that it was the motives of the person taking any action which made them good or bad. He saw hell as a state of alienation from God, and his understanding of God as Being itself, existing beyond time and space, led him to see eternal life as something quite different from everlasting time. It exists out of time.

But there was a high price to be paid for all this. Very often his views had been developed in response to a contrary view which he felt he had to challenge, whether it was Arianism, Donatism or Pelagianism. But the ideas of Arius, Donatus and Pelagius were neither entirely wrong nor entirely unreasonable. Each was an understandable response to genuine problems, and many conscientious Christians followed their teaching in good faith.

Viewed from the position of the twenty-first century there was plenty of room for compromise, for differences of emphasis, and even for acceptance that different people see things differently and would ideally try to understand each other rather than leap to condemnation of anything other than their own beliefs. But it is characteristic of mankind to want to be right about things, and in each case Augustine and his opponents adopted extreme opposed positions, and that led to unfortunate consequences.

His teaching about the trinity, which arose from his opposition to Arianism, led eventually to the adoption of the *filioque* clause, thus contributing to the schism between what became the Greek Orthodox Church of the east and the separate Latin Catholic Church of the west. It also led to the drawing up of the Athanasian Creed, which, however cleverly it defines the doctrine of the trinity, is above all notable for its preliminary and final words, asserting that anyone who does not believe the catholic faith whole and undefiled will perish everlastingly.

His opposition to Donatism, for all the merits of his inclusive view of the Christian community and his affirmation of the Catholic view of the validity of the sacraments, led to the justification of the use of force to compel conformity of belief. His teaching against Pelagianism, which had the great merit that it was based on an acknowledgement of the majesty of God compared to the weakness and sinfulness of Man, tended to destroy the concept of free will and seemed to lead logically to the idea of predestination, whose harshness is difficult to reconcile with the idea of a loving God. His teaching about original sin led to an unhealthy view of sexual matters in the church over the following centuries and, hand in hand with that, a view of women which caused them to be seen both as a source of sexual temptation to men and as intrinsically inferior.

That view of things helped to exacerbate the problem of men seeing women not only as inferior to themselves but also as chattels to be used, despite the evidence of Jesus's attitude and Paul's clear assertion to the contrary. At the same time sin came to be seen as primarily something sexual. Failings such as pride, anger, sloth and gluttony have often been ignored, and the very words "sin" and "immorality" came eventually to be widely applied exclusively to sexual misdemeanours, with which Jesus does not appear to have been much concerned.

The accumulated damage of all that has to be weighed in the balance against the merits of Augustine's thought and his teaching. His greatness is in no doubt. He was the first really important western theologian writing in Latin since Tertullian, and there was no thinker to match him for at least six hundred years, and possibly longer. He produced a synthesis of Christian theology in *The City of God* which dominated the official teaching of the church for at least a thousand years and his ideas have continued to be a powerful influence down to the present day.

Augustine also had the great merit that he knew he could be wrong. Throughout his life he was struggling to understand better. Sometimes he knew that he believed a particular view to be mistaken but did not necessarily know what should replace it. Late in life he published a work in which he reconsidered many of his earlier writings, withdrawing some of his earlier opinions and correcting others. He was anxious not to be regarded as an authority and believed that it would damage the faith if people accepted his opinions simply because it was he who had expressed them. Nevertheless, his ideas were to dominate the Catholic Church in the west for at least the next thousand years, and in many ways, for good or ill, his influence on thinking within the church is still powerful.

Chapter 6

Benedict, Anselm and Peter Abelard

The breakdown of the Roman Empire in the west resulted in a world torn by warfare. The *Pax Romana* no longer provided security, the Roman economy in the west disintegrated, and trade between one place and another could no longer be relied upon. One way to survive in this dangerous world was to form small, self-sufficient communities with groups of men from all walks of life, and later groups of women as well, who came together, not only to find a way of surviving in a dangerous world, but also seeking to remember the past, worship God and maintain a level of literacy which would enable them to read the scriptures and, for example, the writings of the Early Fathers of the Church.

One of these groups, living in what came to be called a monastery, was established on a mountain called Monte Cassino, half way between Naples and Rome. It was led by Benedict of Nursia, who had been born in about 480, fifty years after the death of Augustine and four after the deposition of the last Roman emperor in the west, Romulus Augustulus. Benedict wrote what he described as "a little rule for beginners" about how to live in such a community. It was no more than roughly twelve thousand words long (today it would conveniently fit into a booklet of thirty to forty pages), and provided detailed instructions on how to conduct the regular worship of God and how to maintain discipline among the members, who were known as monks. It exhibits the Roman virtues of reason, moderation and stability, and it was also permeated with Christian thinking, clearly inspired by the teaching of Jesus on how to live.

Later it was known as *The Rule of St Benedict*. It is in no way scholarly or intellectual, except in so far as it is peppered with scriptural quotations. It is simple, clear and straightforward, providing a remarkably wise, humane and authoritative explanation of how to live a communal Christian life. It is also practical, explaining how a monastery should be self-sufficient, with water, a mill, a garden and provision for domestic crafts, so that the monks would not have to leave the boundaries of the monastic lands.

Its wisdom is striking. For example, Benedict prescribes that when any important business needs to be done, the abbot should ask the advice of the whole community, "for God often reveals what is better to the younger", but then, having heard their advice and considered it, he needs to use his own judgement and "dispose all things with prudence and justice". It is advice which could well be followed with advantage by people running organisations and institutions today, and sometimes is.

The rule requires strict discipline. The monks were not allowed to have any property of their own, they met communally for worship seven times in each twenty-four-hour period, both by day and at night, and they were required to be engaged in manual labour and in sacred reading at specified hours. They were not to eat any meat. They were expected to speak only when necessary, and never after Compline, the last of the seven services of the day. They slept clothed, always ready to rise without delay.

The arrangements made for maintaining discipline could in the right hands be very effective. A monk who broke the rule would be privately rebuked. If he repeated the offence, he would be rebuked privately a second time. The next step was to rebuke him publicly, after that to require him to eat his meals alone, and then to work alone. Someone who still would not mend his ways could be subjected to corporal punishment, and finally, if neither that nor repeated prayers could get him to reform, he would be expelled from the monastery.

It was strict, but also humane. The abbot would send "old and prudent brethren" to comfort someone who had been condemned to eat or work alone, and they would see if they could persuade him to seek the abbot's pardon. Meanwhile the abbot himself was under an obligation to do everything he could to bring a stray sheep back to the fold. The humanity of the rule is also seen in the careful arrangements for the care of the sick, which begin with the words, "Before all things and above all things care must be taken of the sick, so that they may be served in very deed as Christ himself, for he said: 'I was sick and ye visited me, and what ye did to one of these least ones, ye did unto me'". Arrangements were made for a special room and "an attendant who is God-fearing, diligent and careful", and the rule against eating meat was relaxed for those who were sick.

A portion of the rule, which was divided up into a hundred and thirty-three sections, was read aloud each day during meal times, so that the whole rule was read through publicly three times a year. A section was usually a passage of between a hundred and two hundred words, but sometimes as few as twenty-five, and never more than about three hundred. Meanwhile in daily worship all one hundred and fifty psalms were recited or chanted every week, and any monk living at Monte Cassino would before long know thoroughly both the rule and the psalms. The scriptures were read both privately and publicly.

Monte Cassino came to be seen as a model of the monastic life, and one community after another sought a copy of the rule, which spread in the way that Jesus had said the Kingdom of Heaven spread, like yeast leavening bread or like a tiny mustard seed which grew into a tree large enough for the birds to come and roost in its branches. No arrangements were made for any organisation tying monasteries together. But bit by bit, over the next few hundred years, more and more monasteries governed by *The Rule of St Benedict* spread all over western Europe. Life according to the rule influenced the monks, and many of those monks influenced the world around them.

All this was happening during the second half of the first millennium, the period of history often referred to as the Dark Ages. The barbarian tribes which had flooded into the empire had mostly come not to destroy it but to share in all that the empire had to offer, which included Christianity. So over those centuries Western Europe came to be divided into bishoprics and the bishoprics in turn were divided into parishes. It was an agricultural and largely illiterate world in which parish priests usually came from much the same background as their parishioners, to whom they probably taught the Lord's Prayer and perhaps also the Ten Commandments which Moses had enjoined on the confederation of Hebrew tribes which he led out of slavery in Egypt. Some priests probably repeated to their flock a number of the parables told by Jesus, such as the stories of the Good Samaritan and the Prodigal Son, and they may have told them about the Sermon on the Mount. But it is difficult to know. There is no record of such things, and the sermon was not a normal mode of communication at that time.

Almost certainly they told them something of the Christmas and Easter stories. Churches were often decorated in bright colours, with pictures of saints and of the Day of Judgement, with the righteous ascending to a heaven inhabited by angels, and the damned descending into a hell inhabited by demons, and that pictorial declaration of the difference between Good and Evil gradually produced the view that heaven was a physical place up in the sky and hell similarly a physical place under the ground.

From the beginning Christianity had always involved an interaction between the material and the spiritual. For almost all Christians the most important symbols of the divine were bread and wine. However much they disagreed with each other about just what they meant by that, there was a sense in which they were united in seeing the bread and the wine as symbols of the God they worshipped. The western area of what we now call Europe was in those centuries overwhelmingly an agricultural society, and throughout that society priests tried to find simple ways of conveying both the teaching of Jesus and what were assumed to be the generally accepted beliefs of Christianity. Various simplified versions of the Nicene Creed were used at baptisms, and during the eighth century what is now known as the Apostles' Creed came to be generally accepted.

The Apostles' Creed, whose name is misleading, since it was written some six or seven hundred years after the time of the apostles, omits much of the theological detail of the Nicene Creed. It includes the *filioque* clause as a consequence of Augustine's insistence that the Holy Spirit proceeds from the Son as well as from the Father, and another addition is a reference to Jesus descending into hell in the time between his crucifixion and resurrection to give those already dead a chance of salvation. That, like the pictures on the wall, tended to confirm the idea of hell as a place inhabited by demons under the earth.

Christian ideas got mixed with tribal customs, and the teaching of Jesus, the ideas of his followers, and some awareness of Greek philosophy all influenced the way people lived. Pagan festivals were changed into Christian feast days, with the midwinter festival chosen as the day on which to celebrate the birth of Jesus, and pagan temples were consecrated as Christian churches. There seems to have been little thinking about theology other than in monasteries, but the life of Western Europe gradually became less barbaric and more civilized and eventually emerged into what historians call the twelfth-century renaissance.

Meanwhile some strange ideas came to be accepted. For example, one view of the doctrine of the incarnation, the idea that the Word, the *logos*, took human form and dwelt among us as Jesus, was influenced by something characteristic of early feudal relationships. Fighting men, or knights, would commend themselves to a powerful baron in an agreement of mutual support. The knight would serve the baron, who in return was expected to be a good lord to the knight, who was now his vassal, and would support him in times of need. In most of Europe it was not necessarily a permanent relationship. A vassal could throw off his allegiance to his lord (that is, defy him – a process known as *diffidatio*) and commend himself to another lord. Issues of loyalty sometimes clashed with the practicalities of power.

That came to be applied to the way in which the incarnation was explained. God, it was suggested, was faced with the problem that Man, ever since the time of Adam and the Fall and Adam and Eve's expulsion from the Garden of Eden, had thrown off the allegiance he owed to God and defied Him. He had voluntarily subjected himself to the Devil and could not be freed from that subjection without a breach of justice. But God found a way out of this problem by taking human form as Jesus of Nazareth. The Devil then managed to have him crucified, but since Jesus was innocent, the Devil forfeited his right to justice. God the Father could now accept the allegiance of those who were willing to be faithful to Him. He had cleverly tricked the Devil. It is not an explanation which would commend itself to anyone today, for none of us lives in a social and political environment in which it makes any sense. It was, however, how some men in the tenth century naturally thought.

In that dangerous world, in which most men worked in the fields and in which a horse-riding upper class of fighting men defended them from Northmen, Saracens and Magyars, some monasteries were oases of learning and spirituality. The work of the monks included recovering and copying out the writings of the ancient world, such as the works of Aristotle, the works of the Early Fathers of the Church, and above all the Bible. That work was thought of not as scholarship but as manual labour, the *opus manum*. While some monks worked in the field, another tended bees, and another made shoes, there were usually some at work in the *scriptorium* making an illuminated copy of the Bible. For centuries they recorded very little that was new.

Some new thinking did go on in monasteries, and a particularly striking example from the middle of the ninth century is two treatises on eucharistic theology received by Charlemagne's grandson, King Charles the Bald of France, from the monastery of Corbie in the north of France. The abbot set out the case for transubstantiation, the idea that at the moment of consecration the "substance" of the bread and wine changed into the "substance" of the actual body and blood of Christ, while the "accidents", the physical characteristics, remained the same. The other treatise was by another monk of Corbie, who argued that the sacraments should be seen as memorials of Christ's passion, and that any divine presence was spiritual and in no way physical. The fact that these two treatises were sent to the king together indicates that at this time it was still entirely acceptable for two monks living in the same monastery to hold quite different views on the nature of the sacraments and remain in fellowship with each other.

It was not until the eleventh century that the first really significant thinker about Christianity for centuries emerged in the west. The life and work of Anselm, who was born in or near Aosta in the Italian Alps in about 1033, marks the beginning of a flowering of monastic philosophy and theology which became an important part of the twelfth-century renaissance. As a young man in his late twenties Anselm left home to go to the monastery of Bec in Normandy, where a fellow countryman of his from Pavia called Lanfranc had established a reputation as a scholar and teacher. Lanfranc was the prior, the abbot's deputy, at Bec, and Anselm went there to be taught by him.

Meanwhile, as government became more than a matter of fighting and imposing the will of a tribal leader, or king, on his subjects by force, the monasteries were a resource from which rulers were able to find literate and able men to aid them in the business of government. Many an abbot or his deputy, the prior, was called from his monastery to be a bishop and take part in the business of government, and in the tenth and eleventh centuries the monasteries were increasingly providing the bishops and statesmen of western Christendom.

In Normandy, for example, Duke William in 1063 summoned the distinguished scholar Lanfranc from being the prior of Bec to be the abbot of his newly founded monastery of St Stephen's, Caen, and then in 1070, by which time William was king of England, he appointed Lanfranc as Archbishop of Canterbury. It was a position of enormous responsibility, for when William returned to the continent to fight, it was Lanfranc whom he left in charge of the government of England. Meanwhile the position of pope was often filled by a monk, and in the thirty-six years from 1073 until 1119, five popes in succession, Gregory VII, Victor III, Urban II, Paschal II and Gelasius II, were all monks.

That was at the time of the so-called Investiture Contest of the late eleventh and early twelfth centuries, which was primarily about the issue of whether or not ecclesiastical appointments should be made by laymen. The German emperor and the kings of, for example, France and England, could not afford to give up the right to appoint to bishoprics the men they needed for governing their countries. But Pope Gregory VII asserted that appointments to ecclesiastical positions by laymen, even by the emperor or by a king, were not just inappropriate but sinful.

The controversy tore Western Europe apart for fifty years, and when a compromise was eventually reached, it was on the basis that the emperor or king could decide on an appointment, but the newly chosen bishop would then be invested with his insignia of office by the pope or other bishops. The reality of power remained with the monarch, but the symbolism of investiture remained the prerogative of the Church, and it was in that sense that the papacy claimed to have won the Investiture Contest.

In 1070, three years before Gregory VII became Pope, Anselm had succeeded Lanfranc as prior of Bec, and fifteen years later, by which time he was forty-five, he was chosen as abbot. After Lanfranc's death in 1089 the then King of England, Willian Rufus, kept the position of Archbishop of Canterbury vacant for four years, in order to collect the revenues himself, but in 1093, thinking that he was dying, he decided to atone for his sins by making the most famously holy abbot in Europe archbishop, and appointed Anselm. Lanfranc had been an outstanding Archbishop of Canterbury, and Anselm was never able to match him in that role, but though Lanfranc had previously been a renowned scholar and teacher, his former pupil, Anselm, was unquestionably the greater thinker.

During the time when Anselm was at Bec he wrote two famous works, the first of which is the *Monologion*, which is a monologue, or meditation, on the reason for Faith. In its preface he makes the point that he will never appeal to scripture or any authority to justify his argument. He will rely entirely on Reason. That in itself is an extraordinary break with the tradition of centuries of justifying everything by appealing to authority, and particularly biblical authority. He begins the meditation by observing that there are things that are good all around us, and from that he goes on to assert that there must be something supremely good. Eventually he draws the conclusion that the supremely good thing must be responsible for the existence of everything else, and that God, having the attribute of supreme goodness, must be that Being.

Just how extraordinary was his decision to rely entirely on Reason and not appeal to scriptural authority can be seen from the fact that his former teacher, Lanfranc, criticised the *Monologion* precisely because he disapproved of the lack of any appeals to scripture and authority. Lanfranc, in the terms of his own time, had been a renowned teacher, but as a philosopher he was not in the same class as his pupil, Anselm, who has come to be seen as the originator or father of medieval scholasticism.

The other work of significance written by Anselm while he was at Bec was the *Proslogion*, a meditation on the nature of God, whose title simply means "Discourse". Anselm probably called it that to go with *Monologion*, which is a pity, because its original working title, *Fides quaerens intellectum*, or "Faith seeking understanding", sets out the essence of Anselm's approach to these matters. "I do not seek to understand that I may believe", he wrote, "but I believe that I may understand", and while believing he tried to demonstrate the truth of the Faith by Reason and not by quoting authorities.

We are so used to the assumption that thought progresses either by logical deduction or by drawing conclusions from observation that it is difficult to appreciate that in the early Middle Ages the characteristic mode of thought was by appealing to authority – to the scriptures, or to Pliny or Aristotle. Nowadays almost the only area of intellectual life where appeal to authority still trumps all else is in the assertions of fundamentalists, whether Christian, Jewish, Islamic or Atheist. Anselm had broken away from that a thousand years ago.

The *Proslogion* includes one of Anselm's greatest intellectual achievements, which is now known as the ontological argument for the existence of God, because ontology is the modern name for the study of the nature of being. In the Middle Ages it was simply spoken of as *ratio Anselmi*, or "Anselm's reason", and it was not intended by him as a proof. Rather, it was a meditation set out in writing.

Anselm took as his starting point the opening words of psalm 14: "The foolish man has said in his heart, there is no God". He went on to ask what, in this context, was meant by the concept of God, and he decided that it must be *aliquid quo maior nihil cogitari potest*, or "that than which nothing greater can be thought". This led eventually to the proposition that a God which existed *in re*, "in reality", as well as *in intellectu*, "in the mind", must be greater than a God which existed only *in intellectu*, and from that to the conclusion that God must therefore exist.

An early objection took the form of proposing a parallel argument. Imagine an island so big that no greater island can be thought. That island exists in the imagination, and according to Anselm's reasoning, it was suggested, an even greater one must exist in reality, which is absurd. But Anselm did not assert a general principle that something which exists in reality is always going to be greater than that which exists only in the imagination. His argument applies solely and exclusively to the idea of a divine being, and the argument has such force that it still seemed impressive to the non-Christian philosopher Bertrand Russell in the twentieth century.

Russell describes in his autobiography how he was walking down Trinity Lane in Cambridge one morning when he threw his tobacco tin up in the air and caught it again, exclaiming, "Great Scot! The ontological argument is sound". And it is sound once one has conceded the point at the start that God is "that than which nothing greater can be thought". But conceding that means that in the last resort it is a circular argument. Despite that it is probably the nearest anyone has ever come to finding appropriate words to express something worthwhile about the nature of God. It is not so tied to any description, picture or myth that those things get in the way of understanding, and it is questionable whether anyone has ever improved on it.

Anselm was sixty years old when he was brought from Bec to Canterbury, and it was while he was Archbishop of Canterbury that he produced an explanation of the incarnation which is widely regarded as his greatest work: the *Cur Deus Homo*, or "Why a God-Man?" It is in the form of a dialogue rather than a meditation, as were the *Monologion* and the *Proslogion*, and it offers a novel explanation of the doctrine of the incarnation. That is, Anselm explains in a new way why God took human flesh in the person of Jesus. The explanation current at the time was the idea that Man had thrown off his allegiance to God and subjected himself to the Devil, with God then tricking the Devil into forfeiting his right to justice and sacrificing Jesus on the cross. It did not seem to Anselm to make sense.

His alternative begins with the proposition that Man was created by God for eternal blessedness. By his sinfulness Man seemed to have frustrated God's purpose. But it is impossible for the will of God to be frustrated, so there had to be some means of redemption. What was needed was an offering which outweighed Man's disobedience. Such an offering ought to be made by Man, but only God was good and great enough to make it. Therefore, it had to be made by someone who was both God and Man. Therefore, the Incarnation was necessary. So "the Word was made flesh and dwelt among us". Jesus lived on Earth as a man. That was not just something which a loving God did to help human beings. It was needed in order to fulfil the purpose of creation, and Jesus died as "a full, perfect and sufficient sacrifice for the sins of the whole world".

In the six hundred years from the death of Augustine till the birth of Anselm Western Europe had been transformed. Its economy had grown in an entirely different way from that which had characterised the Roman Empire. It was less urban, more agricultural, less dependent on trade and more geared to self-sufficiency. But by the eleventh century trade was reviving, water and wind power were being developed, and there were new developments in building techniques and in military technology. Towns were growing. Artistic tastes were changing. New ideas were spreading.

During Anselm's long lifetime of nearly eighty years (he died in 1109) those changes continued. Cathedrals were being built in the developing towns, and in the twelfth century intellectual life shifted increasingly from the monasteries to the schools, later known as universities, which grew up attached to cathedrals. There schoolmen, who were secular clergy rather than monks, worked at discovering, translating and writing down the works of the great thinkers of the past, and although little was original, they were laying the foundations of future scholarship, and young men with a zeal for learning could travel from place to place and learn from masters, who were no longer necessarily bishops or monks, and without needing to become monks themselves.

One of these wandering scholars was Peter Abelard, who possessed the most original mind of all the twelfth-century schoolmen, and who studied, argued and made his reputation at the school attached to the cathedral church of Notre Dame in Paris. He turned Anselm's concept of faith seeking understanding about and thought in terms of understanding leading on to faith. He saw doubt as a virtue. Doubting would lead to enquiry. Enquiry would lead to truth. He influenced any number of young men. He encouraged them to think by setting out for them a series of conflicting authorities in his great teaching manual *Sic et Non* which means "Yes and No", and challenging them to resolve the conflicts. He did not tell them what the answers were. He was getting them to think for themselves. It was something of an educational revolution.

Abelard was from the ruling class (his father was a knight in Brittany) and as a young man he had to choose whether to be a knight or a monk or a secular clerk. He chose the latter, and then had to decide whether to study the classics, logic, law or theology, aiming for a career in teaching or in working for the lay power or for the church or both. He opted for logic and theology and also for teaching. Like Anselm he had the courage to think creatively in a world in which doctrine was something passed down through the centuries and usually accepted without discussion.

While the scholarship of the eleventh century had brought the work of the Early Fathers of the Church to the attention of scholars, it was Abelard who faced the fact that they disagreed. In his brilliant preface to *Sic et Non* he explains that "some of the opinions of even the saints appear not only to differ from one to another but actually to be in conflict", and he took the view that one had to face the fact that some of them must be wrong. That was bad enough. He went further and subjected traditional doctrine to criticism based on reasoning and rational criticism, and one side-effect of his work was that the meaning of the word *theologia*, or "theology", changed from a study specifically of the nature of God to the study of the whole range of Christian doctrine.

His fame as a teacher resulted in one of the canons of Notre Dame, Fulbert, employing him to teach his niece, Heloise, of whom Abelard said in his *Historia Calamitatum*, which is an account of a whole series of disasters in his life, that she was "a lady of no mean appearance, while in literary excellence she was the first". He and Heloise fell in love, spent their lesson time in making love, had a baby and got married secretly, because, since Abelard was a canon of Sens cathedral, it would have been damaging to his career for the marriage to be made public. Then thugs employed by Fulbert attacked and castrated Abelard, and the marriage was dissolved in the only way then possible: both of them entered religious houses, he to continue writing and teaching, she eventually to become a distinguished abbess.

Abelard can seem peculiarly modern – almost the first modern man one encounters in the Middle Ages. He protested against extended acts of penitence, which were too often seen as payment for sin. Of what value were they unless one was genuinely sorry about that for which they were undertaken? At the same time, he was against the sort of penitential hymns which had become popular, with words like "Sighing we make our prayer. Pardon, O Lord, our sins" or "Receive with kindness, Lord, our weeping and our song". He wanted neither external acts nor emotional gush, but true inner sorrow for sin – and some scholars believe that it was this view of Abelard's that led eventually to the practice of individual confession.

He was strongly committed to the belief that sin was a matter of intention. A man was not a sinner simply because what he did was objectively wrong, nor even because he felt sinful desires. Sin was a matter of giving consent to those sinful desires. Thus Abelard started a shift in Christian understanding of sin from the idea that it was what you did that mattered to the idea that the really important thing was what you intended. He saw that deeds in themselves are morally neutral. What is sinful is choosing to do something knowing it to be wrong. In his inimitable fashion he was prepared to face the consequences of his views when applied to difficult cases. Thus he shocked the saintly abbot Bernard of Clairvaux by arguing that those who crucified Jesus were not sinning if they believed that they were acting rightly. Abelard had come to much the same conclusion as Augustine had more than seven hundred years earlier about the significance of intention, but Augustine's thinking in this area had been neglected.

It was Abelard who gave the medieval world the idea of a God who loves rather than judges mankind and who, in the incarnation, entered into sympathetic understanding of mankind and, by suffering on the cross, offered salvation to all. The hymns he wrote stress the importance of compassion. Mankind, he pointed out, had before them the example of Jesus suffering and dying on the cross, and Christians needed to respond to that with compassion and a sense of awe, admiration, sorrow and gratitude for what Jesus had undergone. He followed Anselm in denying that the crucifixion was a price paid to the devil to release mankind from servitude to sin. God owed the devil nothing. Jesus had gone to the cross as a practical example of his own teaching.

Abelard saw the crucifixion as the supreme example of divine love, and his view of God and his insight into divine love probably owe a lot to Heloise, to his love for her and to her love for him. The crucified Christ is seen by Abelard as suffering in agony rather than ruling from the cross in majesty as *Christus Victor*, and the crucifixion was also seen by Abelard as a continuation of Jesus's teaching, for on the cross, wrote Abelard, Jesus taught us "by both word and example even to the point of death, thus binding us to himself in love".

Abelard was a brilliant teacher, logician, philosopher, theologian, hymn writer and even autobiographer. He was also famous for his love affair with Heloise, and later those who knew him admired him as a monk. He continued all his life to write with original insight on such topics as the doctrine of the trinity, no doubt straying in and out of heresy in the process. But the reason that Bernard of Clairvaux attacked him at the Council of Sens in 1140 and had his writings on the trinity condemned as heretical and burnt was above all that Bernard saw him as the equivalent of someone who nowadays would get his name in the Sunday papers, guilty of a scandalous love affair and guilty of pride, setting out his clever ideas in order to be admired. Bernard was not against reason and a rational approach to doctrine, but he was against Abelard, whom he believed to be both a sinner and too clever by half.

Anselm and Abelard in their different ways mark a high point in Christian thinking, symbolised in the case of Anselm by the idea of Faith seeking Understanding, and in the case of Abelard by the idea of Understanding leading on to Faith. Both spent most of their lives as monks, living under obedience to *The Rule of St Benedict*, influenced, as was so much of the world in which they lived, by the simplicity, humanity and spirituality of the rule, rooted as it was in the teaching and thinking of Jesus of Nazareth.

Chapter 7

Thomas Aquinas, William of Ockham and John Wyclif

The first century of the second millennium, during which both Anselm and Abelard were born, was a time when a significant reform movement in the west involved an attack on the widespread practices of clerical marriage and what was called simony. The attack on clerical marriage was both because of a belief that hands which handled the sacraments should not be sullied by contact with women, and also because of the danger that ecclesiastical offices might come to be inherited. Simony was the sin of treating spiritual things as commodities to be bought and sold. The name comes from the story in the eighth chapter of the Acts of the Apostles, in which a man called Simon, later referred to as Simon Magus, or Simon the Magician, offered the apostles money to give him the power to bestow the Holy Spirit. Peter gave him short shrift for thinking that a divine gift could be purchased with money.

A thousand years later the Roman church was asserting its authority against that of the lay power and extending the definition of simony to include all lay participation in ecclesiastical appointments. For centuries, as kings, barons and knights had extended their power, they had arranged for the building of churches in local communities, and some of them had founded monasteries. They often expected to appoint the priest who administered the sacraments in a church they had had built, and they expected to be involved in the election of the abbot of a monastery which they or their forebears had founded.

The verb "to elect" simply meant "to choose". How that "election" or "choosing" was done varied. At the same time kings appointed bishops. All this Pope Gregory VII in the late eleventh century declared to be sinful, and it resulted in the clash which is known as the Investiture Conflict because the compromise of 1122, which ended the main conflict between the German emperor in the west and the pope and is known as the Concordat of Worms, involved the papacy in conceding the right of appointment of a bishop to the emperor, while the emperor conceded the right of investment to the pope.

That century, which was just beginning, saw many new developments, including new experiments in monasticism, of which the most significant was probably the rise of the Cistercian Order, which was more ascetic than many Benedictine houses, and one of whose most outstanding figures was Bernard of Clairvaux. The end of the twelfth century saw the pontificate of Innocent III, which marks the apogee of papal power in the Middle Ages, and the founding of two orders of friars, the Franciscans and the Dominicans, who, instead of living in a monastery, would go from place to place, preaching, hearing confessions and offering spiritual guidance.

The cathedral schools of the twelfth century were developing into what we call universities, and by the mid-thirteenth century an attempt was being made to clarify what were acceptable beliefs as well as what behaviour was or was not acceptable to the church authorities. Some scholars were trying to find an all-embracing theological system, covering everything that Christians should believe. Others were developing an all-embracing system of canon law, covering everything about how Christians should behave.

Some monks, like the schoolmen attached to cathedrals, were now seriously involved in scholarship, and before long members of the two new orders of friars were also to be found studying at the universities. Thomas Aquinas, a Dominican who lived in the middle of the thirteenth century, from 1225 until 1274, studied at Paris. William of Ockham, a Franciscan who lived from 1287 until 1347, studied at Oxford.

Theology was by now seen not only as the study of God but also as the study of everything to do with His relationship to creation. Canon law was, and still is, a legal system for regulating morals and religious practices and structures. At the beginning of the twelfth century there was no clear distinction between theology and canon law. It was only as each of them was codified that a distinction emerged between what the church expected Christians to believe, regulated by theology, and how it expected them to behave, which was regulated by canon law.

By about the time that Peter Abelard died in 1142 a monk called Gratian working in Bologna was drawing up a collection of canon law cases intended as a guide to decision-making on all matters moral and spiritual. When Pope Gregory IX in 1234 issued the first set of papal decretals, or edicts, as a supplement to it, the church had a collection of answers to all, or more or less all, problems of human behaviour.

Shortly after this Thomas Aquinas was trying to do much the same for theology at the university of Paris. By his time much of Aristotle had been re-discovered, translated and subjected to careful thought and criticism by Muslim, Christian and Jewish scholars, and Aquinas now set out to reconcile Aristotle with Christianity and unite Reason with Faith. In 1266, when he was just over forty, he began to write the *Summa Theologica*, which is a detailed account of the main elements of Christian thinking as it was understood at the time. By his death in 1274 he had developed a complete, coherent and remarkably durable theological system.

Between them Gratian and Aquinas had created the ideological framework for the church as a totalitarian society – that is, a society in which those in authority would expect to exercise their authority over every aspect of human thought and behaviour. What was missing, fortunately, was the power to enforce the ideology.

The *Summa Theologica* was a massive and remarkable achievement, which is divided into three parts. The first is concerned with God the Creator, the second with the relationship of Man to God, and the third with the question of how Christ brings about Man's salvation. Throughout it, Aquinas worked on the assumption that the Christian faith is rational – not that its truth can be demonstrated or proved beyond doubt, but rather that, while ultimately it is a response to something beyond Reason, it is not inconsistent with Reason.

One of the most important aspects of his reasoning is what are called the Five Ways, which are all arguments for the existence of God. Aquinas believed that the world mirrored its creator, so it would make sense to look to the world for evidence for the existence of God. He did so, and produced five related arguments which can be relatively easily summarised.

First, he pointed out, everything must have a cause, and he argued from that that there must be an original cause for everything. That original cause is God. Secondly (and this argument is closely related to the first one), causes have effects, or consequences, and he argued that all those consequences can be traced back to the one original cause of everything, namely God. The third argument is that we, Mankind, exist only because some other being brought us into existence, and that other being is God. The fourth argument is that values, such as truth and goodness, must come from somewhere and, he claimed, their origin is from God. The fifth argument, which modern theologians call the teleological argument, is that there are all sorts of things in the world which look as if they have been very cleverly designed. The designer is God.

These five arguments are, of course, all closely related. None of them proves the existence of God, and Aquinas did not say that they did. He was simply arguing that, taking them all together, they suggest that it is perfectly reasonable to believe in the existence of God. He also appreciated the problem that human words are inadequate to describe something like God. He would have been in sympathy with the point made by the twentieth-century philosopher Wittgenstein that, if human words cannot describe the aroma of coffee, they are clearly inadequate to describe God.

Aquinas considered how far it makes sense, for example, to describe God as Father. The point of doing so, he says, is that in some ways God can be seen as like a father: the source of our existence, caring for us and exercising authority over us. But equally there are ways in which He is not like a human father. Above all, He is not a human being. Nor is He necessarily male. Nevertheless, thought Aquinas, the idea of God as Father can be helpful. Similarly, when we say that God is Love, that should not be seen as limiting God to what we, as humans, understand of Love. It must be something far greater than that. But what we understand of Love can act as a pointer towards something beyond our comprehension, which is the Love that is God.

One of the issues to which Aquinas turned his attention was what is called eucharistic theology. Early Christians had met together to eat bread and drink wine in remembrance of their Lord and Saviour, without, so far as one can tell, questioning whether or not anything particular happened to the bread and the wine either before or as they ate and drank. But just as speculation grew about the relationship between Jesus and the Father, and how Jesus could be divine as well as fully human, so speculation grew about what happened to the bread and wine at the eucharist, the regular Sunday service of thanksgiving (it will be remembered that the Greek word *eucharistia* means "thanksgiving").

Much of that speculation rested on the ideas developed in the ancient world by Plato and Aristotle about the existence of a "real" world beyond, or underlying, that which we perceive with our senses, in which there were the *ideas* or *forms* which were the immutable "substances" which underlay those things which we can perceive with our senses. That way of looking at things had survived the collapse of the Roman Empire in the West and had influenced philosophical thinking ever since the time of Plato, who had lived about four hundred years before Christ, and it influenced Aquinas's thinking on eucharistic theology. That is, Aquinas accepted the idea that the "substance" of the bread and wine changed at the moment of consecration into the "substance" of the actual body and blood of Jesus, while their physical characteristics, or "accidents" remained the same. By now this view was called the doctrine of transubstantiation.

Another important aspect of Aquinas's thought is that, like Augustine, he recognised an enormous gulf between God and Man. But that recognition, in itself entirely admirable, led him to develop some strange and complicated ideas. He could not see how God, being as much beyond our comprehension as He is, could ever be directly present in human nature. Yet he also believed that somehow the sinful nature of human beings needed to be changed so that, after death in this life, they could become beings acceptable to God. That led him to the idea that there must be a half-way stage between life on Earth and entry into the Kingdom of Heaven. In that half-way stage a man would acquire a "habit of grace", and then, when he died, the guilt related to his sins would be removed because of the price paid by Jesus on the cross, but he would still, in that half-way house known as purgatory, need to undergo the appropriate punishment for his sins until sufficiently purged to be acceptable to God and capable of being saved.

That is the point at which it makes sense to introduce William of Ockham and his famous razor. Ockham is a village between Woking and Leatherhead in Surrey, just south of the Royal Horticultural Society's gardens at Wisley, and it was probably there that William was born in about 1285, just over ten years after the death of Thomas Aquinas. The so-called razor was his intellectual device for finding the right answer to a problem by cutting out superfluous rubbish. He believed that simplicity was both a theological and a philosophical virtue and took the view that "all things being equal, the simplest solution tends to be the best one".

It seems that William joined the Franciscan Order at the age of fourteen, and ten years later, in 1309, was sent to Oxford to study theology. A good example of the use of his famous razor is his demolition of the complicated explanation Aquinas had postulated about bridging the gulf between God and Man by having a half-way stage of purgatory between this world and the Kingdom of Heaven, in which men, after acquiring a "habit of grace", would undergo punishment for their sins.

William of Ockham simply cut through the complications by saying that God was perfectly capable of accepting a sinner directly, without the need for any intermediate stages. That was so clear and simple that the idea of the "habit of grace" disappears completely, though the church hung on to Aquinas's idea of purgatory, and even today the Roman Catholic church still teaches that those eventually destined for heaven may need to "undergo purification, so as to achieve the holiness necessary to enter the joy of heaven".

Ockham also took issue with Aquinas's arguments for the existence of God. Most particularly, he pointed out that, even if God was the original creator of everything, within which we exist as part of His creation, it does not follow from that that God still exists now. He might have started everything going and then ceased to exist.

A further issue which Ockham considered was the question of what is meant when we say at the beginning of both the Nicene and the Apostles' Creed that we believe in God the Father Almighty. That is, what do we mean by "Almighty" (or *omnipotens*)? It cannot mean that God can do anything now. After all, we know something of the Laws of Nature, we rely on them to be constant, and we do not, or at any rate we should not, expect God to intervene to change them. Another way of putting it is that we expect God to be reliable. As Origen had said, it does not make sense to pray for cool in the heat of summer. The idea of divine omnipotence, said Ockham, must be that God was once free to do anything. He chose to establish a divine order of things which reflects His divine will, and that order will last until the end of time. It is in His nature that He cannot change it.

Ockham distinguished between *potentia absoluta*, or absolute power, which existed before the beginning of time, and *potentia ordinata*, which is what was ordained and so exists now. They represent, he suggested, two different stages in the history of salvation. God could have decided not to create the world. But that is not what happened. He did create it, and having done so, He cannot undo it. That is, in creating it as He did, He limited the options open to Himself, and we have to live with that.

From those examples of the way William of Ockham thought it is not difficult to see that, like Abelard two hundred years earlier, he seriously upset those who accepted the conventional view of things and ignored such matters as the nature of God's omnipotence and whether or not He was still intervening to shape the course of History. But those could be seen as no more than details. What was profoundly upsetting was that William of Ockham challenged the whole grand logical structure built up by St Thomas Aquinas, with its answer to all theological problems. He argued that many of the basic ideas of Christianity could not be proved or demonstrated by logic, but instead had to be accepted by faith, and with his razor he attacked philosophical ideas which had underpinned much of Christian thinking for centuries.

In philosophical terms Aquinas was what is called a Realist, as were more or less all scholars at the time. That is, they accepted the Platonic and Aristotelian ideas about a "real" world underlying that which we can perceive with our senses.

But William of Ockham thought that Plato's and Aristotle's universals, their *ideas* or *forms*, were an unnecessary hypothesis. So he took his razor to something which had been generally accepted by scholars since more than three centuries before Christ and on which much Christian theology was based, and cut it out. He took the view that every individual thing is what it is and no other thing, and that where we see a resemblance among several things we choose to call them by the same name. Thus a horse is a horse because we call it a horse – not because it approximates to the *idea* of "horse" and shares its "substance", or true nature, of "horsiness" with a range of other creatures.

The significance of this view of things, which was not entirely new in William of Ockham's time but was developed by him to the point at which it was seen to be undermining Realism, came to be known by philosophers as Nominalism. It is a view which destroys the rational basis of the idea that Jesus was *homoousion toi patri*, since, if the whole idea of "substance" is misguided, then Jesus can hardly be "of one substance with the Father". Similarly, it destroys the intellectual basis on which was built the doctrine of transubstantiation. If bread and wine do not have a "substance", the bread and wine used in the Eucharist cannot rationally be said to change "substantially" into the actual flesh and blood of Jesus, while the "accidents" remain the same.

Nevertheless, William of Ockham did not deny that the bread and wine consecrated in the Eucharist became the body and blood of Christ. He only argued that it could not be justified rationally. It was a divine mystery which had to be accepted by faith. All the same, once transubstantiation was widely seen as intellectually unsound, it was no very big step from that to the view that the bread and the wine of the Eucharist should be seen simply as symbols of the body and blood of Christ, which should be eaten and drunk as an act of remembrance, or *anamnesis*, aiming to bring the past effectively into the present, rather than as sacraments offered to God by a priest as part of a continuing, or repeated, sacrifice.

In 1324, when nearly forty, William of Ockham was, not surprisingly, charged with heresy and summoned to appear at the papal court, which was then at Avignon in the south of France, to answer the charges against him. While he was there and writing about theology, he got involved in a dispute between the Franciscan order and the papacy about the idea of "apostolic poverty". The Franciscans had developed the belief that their way of life was a special form of the imitation of Christ, and their attachment to the rule of poverty led them to a general condemnation of the ownership of property.

In 1323, a year before William of Ockham was accused of heresy, Pope John XXII had denounced the Franciscan view of poverty as heresy, and consequently, since William was in Avignon, the head of the Franciscan Order asked him to investigate the issue. William concluded that it was the pope who was teaching heresy and, indeed, that the pope was himself a heretic. Again, it is not surprising that William of Ockham was now excommunicated. He spent the remaining years of his life abroad under the protection of the Holy Roman emperor, who was also at odds with the pope.

Through most of the fourteenth century the papacy was established at Avignon, apparently under the control of the French king. This period, when the papal court was at Avignon, was referred to by the poet Petrarch as "the Babylonish Captivity", in a reference to the time when the leaders of the Kingdom of Judah had been taken into captivity in Babylon. The period when the pope was in Avignon and there was no pope in Rome was followed by a further period at the end of the fourteenth century and early in the fifteenth century in which there were two popes – one still in Avignon and another back in Rome. At about the same time Europe also experienced the Black Death and widespread fighting.

Civilization seemed to many people to be collapsing, and two consequences of that were that a number of popular religious movements sprang up and that there was widespread criticism of corruption at the head of the church. Europe had become a Christian society and many of the faithful wanted to live good lives. They yearned for some direct experience of Jesus or the Virgin Mary, and were increasingly out of sympathy with the official view of the church that the only way to salvation was through the sacraments administered by priests mediating between ordinary people and God.

There was little or no demand for reform of doctrine. The theological system laid out by Thomas Aquinas and the criticisms of it by William of Ockham were known to scholars but not to the mass of the people, who widely assumed that the church knew what was right and wrong and that it was human frailty which led to inefficiency and human sinfulness which led to corruption. Corruption was particularly abhorrent when it could be detected in the church, and both the wealth and some very obvious corruption in the church acted as a stimulus to an English clergyman and theologian called John Wyclif, who lived from about 1330, by which time William of Ockham was excommunicated and under the protection of the emperor, until 1384.

Wyclif studied at Oxford, where he was briefly Master of Balliol College. He was seen in his own day as a significant philosopher and theologian, though his thinking on such matters was entirely in the scholastic tradition and he remained a Realist, like Aquinas. For example, he taught that the reason the bread and wine of the eucharist did not change "substantially" into the body and blood of Christ was because, as a committed Realist, he believed that their substances could not be altered by a priest chanting some words over them in what was known as the act of consecration. It was not because, like William of Ockham, he would have denied that anything had a "substance".

But the importance of Wyclif does not lie in such matters. It was his zeal for righteousness which was important and led to a range of new and disturbing ideas. Like the Donatists a thousand years earlier, he took the view that sinfulness could so corrupt a man as to invalidate the sacraments administered by him. He believed that the church should abandon its material possessions, and in particular he opposed the payment to the pope of what were known as "annates", which were payments to the pope of one year's income from all ecclesiastical appointments throughout Europe, and which had been levied by the pope since the early fourteenth century. He encouraged the translation of the Bible into English to make it accessible to ordinary people. Finally, he set up a network of poor preachers to go round the country spreading these ideas.

During the later years of his life Wyclif's perception of the fourteenth-century church was that it was made up of "sects", all of which needed to be rooted out. Worst of all was the papal sect, with all the trappings of the papal curia in both Avignon and Rome. Then there were the various religious orders, above all the monks and friars, all of which, Wyclif believed, had put their various rules above the teaching of Christ, and had put obedience to their superiors above obedience to the Gospel, the Good News of Christ.

Wyclif wanted parliament to advise the king to close all monasteries, chantries and hospitals, and any other houses belonging to the various sects, confiscate their land and possessions, and perhaps find employment for any monks and friars who were not entirely corrupt as parish clergy or as schoolmasters. In his own lifetime that seemed to most people an extremist and even a deranged view, but one and a half centuries later, in the reign of Henry VIII, Wyclif's plan for the dissolution of the religious orders was more or less just what happened.

His influence reached far beyond England. Jan Huss, a religious reformer in Bohemia, came into contact with Wyclif's ideas after Anne of Bohemia married Richard II of England. Huss adopted Wyclif's ideas wholesale, and the mixture of those ideas with the Czech nationalism of Bohemia was explosive. It produced a reforming movement which swept Bohemia and whose success was a warning to the rest of the Catholic church in the west of what awaited if it failed to put its house in order.

In 1414 a council met in Constance to try to end the Great Schism, during which, over a period of thirty-six years since 1378, there had been two popes, one in Avignon and one in Rome. Those attending the council also saw it as their task to stamp out heresy and promote reform. Huss was seen as a heretic, but was given a safe-conduct by the emperor to come to the council and put his case. Despite that he was arrested and imprisoned. The emperor was told that heresy was a matter of such importance that the safe-conduct was not valid. Huss was found guilty and burnt to death.

Wyclif was more fortunate. His belief that it was wrong to pay "annates" to Rome found favour during his lifetime with those in power in England, such as John of Gaunt, who was his patron for many years. During his later years he continued writing, arguing that scripture was the ultimate authority for Christianity, that papal claims to authority were unhistorical, and that monasticism was corrupt. He died towards the end of 1384. That was thirty years before the Council of Constance had Jan Huss burnt as a heretic. In 1415 it condemned Wyclif as well and ordered his body and his writings to be burnt. So his body was dug out of consecrated ground, the corpse was burnt and his ashes were scattered on the River Swift.

Already his followers were being repressed. They were contemptuously called Lollards by the authorities, implying that they were mumbling nonsense, and such of them as survived went underground, although not before two had produced an English translation of St Jerome's Vulgate Bible, laboriously copied out by hand before printing presses were available. One consequence of that was that in 1407 all versions of the Bible in English were banned. But some of Wyclif's writings, together with a few copies of the English Bible, survived throughout the fifteenth century, and he came to be described, though who first said it is not known, as "the Morning Star of the Reformation".

Wyclif's thought is less profound than that of Anselm or Abelard, Aquinas or William of Ockham, but its impact on the course of history was probably greater than that of any of them. Similarly, Benedict's ideas back in the early sixth century on how to live a Christian life in a monastery had been in no way profound, but they were important for the age in which he lived, and their clarity, simplicity and wisdom resulted in their having a massive influence on the course of history. Wyclif's entirely different ideas were also important for the age in which he lived, about eight hundred and fifty years later, and his criticisms of the church in the late Middle Ages went on resonating down the coming centuries.

In the first half of the fourteenth century, while William of Ockham was developing his ideas in England, the Ottoman Turks had conquered most of Asia Minor. In the second half of that century, they conquered most of the Balkans. Meanwhile they also adopted the religion of Islam, and about twenty years after the Council of Constance, which lasted from 1414 until 1418, they surrounded and were threatening to take Constantinople. One consequence of that was that in 1439 the Byzantine Emperor John VIII and the Patriarch Joseph of Constantinople accepted union with Rome on behalf of the Orthodox church in the hope of getting military assistance against the Turks. It was a vain hope and, without help from the west, Constantinople fell to the Turks in 1453.

Meanwhile there was passionate opposition throughout what had been the Roman, or Byzantine, Empire to the idea of union with Rome. The feeling was that John VIII and Patriarch Joseph had betrayed them. So the plan for union with Rome collapsed, and thereafter the Orthodox churches of the east survived, tolerated by their Muslim rulers, guarding their orthodoxy, or "correct belief", and maintaining and valuing a tradition of spirituality inherited from the past, but still divided from their fellow Christians in the west, partly by the combination of geography and political realities, but above all by their unwillingness to accept the authority of the pope in Rome.

Back in the west the tradition that ultimate authority in the church was vested in the bishop of Rome, now known as the pope, was well established. He was seen as the successor of the apostle Peter, and asserted his authority as God's representative on Earth. That authority had recently been challenged by what was known as the Conciliar Movement, whose leaders had argued that ultimate authority was vested not in the pope but in the church as a whole, and that important matters of doctrine could only be decided by an ecumenical council. But in 1460, seven years after the fall of Constantinople, Pope Pius II was able to condemn the conciliar doctrine as a "pestilent poison" and assert the theory that the papacy had unlimited and autocratic power.

The papacy appeared to be triumphant, with no one in a position to challenge it. But the papacy itself and the hierarchy of the church of which it was the head both fell far short of the moral standards they theoretically proclaimed. They were seriously open to criticism, and in the late fifteenth century and early sixteenth centuries that criticism was widespread and was building.

Much of the theological thinking of the third century onwards now seems irrelevant when it is compared with the teaching and ideas of Jesus of Nazareth and that of the apostles. But it was in those early centuries of the Christian era that most of the generally accepted beliefs of the Christian church were established, and by the end of the fifteenth century they were generally accepted.

The problem by then was an entirely different one. It was that the behaviour of many of the leaders of the church was clearly in conflict with Jesus's teaching about such things as the abuse of power and excessive love of money. The pope from 1492 until 1503 was Alexander VI, Rodrigo Borgia, who lived a notoriously scandalous life, openly flouting the requirement for clerical celibacy. The next pope, from 1503 until 1513, was Julius II, who made his reputation as a soldier. Two more popes, Leo X, from 1513 until 1521, and Clement VII, from 1523 until 1534, concerned themselves above all with the interests of the Medici family. Corruption in various forms, and above all the abuse of power, was at its worst at the top.

By the early sixteenth century there were people throughout western Christendom demanding reform. What they got was the Reformation.

Chapter 8

Desiderius Erasmus and Martin Luther

One of the outspoken critics of the church as the sixteenth century began was Desiderius Erasmus, who was born in about 1466 and was the second illegitimate son of a Dutch priest called Gerrit and a young woman called Margaret, who took in washing to supplement the family income. Like his father the child was called Gerrit, so his real name was Gerrit Gerritszoon, but he is known to the world as Desiderius Erasmus, the Latin name under which his writings were published. The union of his parents was permanent and was in no way unusual. Although for centuries the western church had sought to stamp out clerical marriage, by the end of the fifteenth century perhaps as many as half the clergy of Western Europe had unofficial wives, or concubines, and often children as well. If marriage was a holy state for laymen, they felt, why should that not be so for priests?

When Gerrit was very young he went with his brother to a school run by a community of the Brethren of the Common Life, who aimed to live simple lives, helping their fellows, and seeking to understand the message of the gospels in a far simpler way from that in which they were studied in universities. He was strongly influenced by their attitude to religion, flourished as a scholar, and developed a passion both for Greek and Roman literature and for the study of the scriptures.

While he was still at school his mother died of the plague and not long afterwards his father died too, so that he was left an orphan at the age of fourteen. He and his brother were urged to enter a monastery, which would provide for them and which also offered the prospect of monastic tranquillity and opportunities for study. The elder brother agreed, but Gerrit had no wish to be a monk and refused until the pressure of poverty at length drove him to enter the Augustinian monastery at Steyn, near Gouda. He took his lifelong vows a year later, and ever afterwards bitterly regretted it.

In 1492, at the age of 26, he was ordained priest and in 1495 was allowed to go to study theology at the University of Paris. He found it stultifying, but before long he was acquiring a reputation for scholarship and as a teacher, and this led to invitations to travel, in particular to England, where he met and was befriended by John Colet, the Dean of St Paul's, Thomas More and Bishop John Fisher. At first his leave of absence from his monastery had been intended to be temporary, but in the event he never returned permanently to Steyn and instead gradually became known as the leader of both classical and biblical scholarship in northern Europe.

In 1516 he published the first Greek text of the New Testament in Western Europe, and he went on to produce a Latin version which corrected many of the mistakes of the translation which had been made in the late fourth century by Eusebius Hieronymus, better known as Jerome, who came from the Roman province of Dalmatia and was a contemporary of Augustine of Hippo. Jerome's version was known as the Vulgate because he translated it out of the original Greek into the common, or vulgar, tongue of Latin. By the sixteenth century it was more than a thousand years old. Erasmus not only produced a new and much more reliable Latin version; he also accompanied it with a commentary. Then in 1517, by which time he was over fifty, he was given papal dispensation from his monastic vows.

Erasmus was teaching that a moral transformation was needed in the church, and the reform he envisaged began with doing away with corruption and scandalous behaviour in high places, for corruption is too often at its worst at the top. Nepotism was rife at the papal curia. The word "nepotism" comes from the Latin word *nepos*, a nephew, and now was very often a euphemism for "bastard", as senior ecclesiastical posts were found for the illegitimate sons of the pope and the cardinals. At the same time simony, the sin of trading in spiritual things, flourished, with ecclesiastical posts being created precisely in order to sell them. Some cardinals held multiple bishoprics and abbacies in much the same way as some modern politicians accumulate a collection of profitable directorships. It was a practice known as "pluralism" and was contrary to canon law. A closely related problem was absenteeism, which was all the more scandalous when cardinals were taking the revenues of bishoprics and abbeys which they never visited.

More than a century earlier Wyclif had attacked corruption in the church with bitter invective. Erasmus had an entirely different approach. He was skilled in the use of irony and mockery to make his point, and was very effective. His book *In Praise of Folly*, written in Latin and first printed as early as 1511, was translated into several languages and was widely read. Inevitably, and despite that lighter touch, he made enemies as well as friends, and the message rang out through Europe loud and clear that there was a need for reform.

Erasmus's call for reform went beyond condemnation of corruption to an attack on what he saw as mechanical religion. He wanted to recover the purity of the Christian message and saw such things as pilgrimages, the purchase of indulgences and the doing of penance as part of a mechanical and legalistic approach to religion, which was just what Christ had inveighed against. It was not that going on a pilgrimage was wrong in itself, or that doing penance was necessarily wrong. But the thinking underlying it was wrong. It was much the same point that Abelard had made four hundred years earlier.

Of course, you might like to visit the Holy Land or Rome, but you should not imagine that by doing so you accumulated merit which would count in your favour on the Day of Judgement. Nor should the leaders of the church deceive you into thinking that way, so that they could themselves make money out of the pilgrim trade. Similarly, if you believe that by reciting *The Lord's Prayer* or *Hail Mary* a given number of times, you are paying the price for some wrong you have done, and which you knew to be wrong, and think that you are then free to repeat the sin so long as you pay the appropriate penance, you are mistaken. The important thing is to be penitent rather than to do penance, and in his translation of Paul's Epistle to the Romans Erasmus altered the traditional Vulgate version "do penance" to "be penitent". There is a world of difference.

Not only was Erasmus against corruption and mechanical religion. He also came to distrust theology. It should be possible, he said, "to have fellowship with the Father, Son and Holy Spirit, without being able to explain philosophically the distinction between them". Eventually, as the Reformation divided Christians against each other, he came to the conclusion that it was desirable to reduce theology to a minimum. What mattered was that Christians should live at peace with one another, and that would only be possible, he believed, if "we define as little as possible". The church had got used to providing an authoritative answer to every question. It was not what Jesus had done, and Erasmus's study of the New Testament made that clear.

But such agnosticism was not acceptable to the papacy, which demanded acceptance of its authority. Nor was it any more acceptable to the other leading reformers, who wanted assurance of truth rather than uncertainty. There was an assumption shared by almost all who concerned themselves with theological and moral issues that there was a right answer to all problems and that they needed to find it. But human beings vary, and they vary in their responses to particular theological views just as they vary in their responses to different political ideas, different music and different painters. Erasmus was ahead of his time in seeing the need for and even the desirability of accepting some variety in human thinking.

It is clear that Erasmus was against corruption, against mechanical forms of religion and against the dogmatism of theologians. But that leaves open the question of what it was he believed in. Most importantly he tells us that the imitation of Christ is more important than correct belief. *Orthopraxis*, or "correct practice", matters more than *orthodoxy*, which is "correct belief". The leaders of the early church had been concerned that its members should look at things as Jesus did, and that they should seek to live like him. They were not concerned with defining the relationship of the Father and the Son – still less with finding an acceptable form of words for the doctrine of the trinity. They rejoiced in following the example and the teaching of their Lord – and so, believed Erasmus, should the people of his own time.

Not only did he believe that it was more important to follow Christ than to have a set of correct beliefs. He also believed that we should meet Christ through the scriptures, and that it was essential for the Bible to be available to ordinary people. "I wish that even the weakest woman should read the gospels and the epistles of Paul", he wrote, "I wish that they were translated into all languages, so that they might be read and understood, not only by Scotchmen and Irishmen but also by Saracens and Turks". That was why he devoted himself throughout his adult life to biblical scholarship – and much Reformation thinking flowed from his provision of a reliable scriptural text.

He looked forward to a thorough reform of society, with men of goodwill throughout Christendom uniting to root out corruption and create a better world. Above all he wanted goodwill – goodwill with a minimum of theology, so that Christians would tolerate differences of opinion, preferably with mutual understanding. As the early Reformation unfolded, the reformers tried to recruit him to their cause. He tried to avoid being drawn into the conflict, but without success, and many reformers came to see him as an enemy because he was not wholeheartedly at one with them.

He retreated to Switzerland, to Basle, then a great centre of Christian humanism. But now the traditionalists saw him as the originator of all the troubles which were affecting the church. Neither side could appreciate that he had no wish to be at enmity with either of them. He simply wanted a reformed church within which men and women could live together in peace and friendship, even when they disagreed. He never abandoned the Catholic church, but he asked to be buried in the Protestant cathedral at Basle, and in 1536, at about the age of seventy, he died, speaking in his native Dutch as he called out for mercy to his "Lieve God". A decade later Pope Paul III described him as "the leader of all the heretics", and called for all his published works to be burnt.

Back in 1517, the year in which Erasmus was given papal dispensation from his monastic vows, the thirty-four-year-old Martin Luther, who was teaching in the local university, had caused uproar when he fixed to the door of the castle church in Wittenberg ninety-five theses setting out his objections to the sale of what were known as indulgences. He was the second son of prosperous peasants (his father was a miner, or mining engineer, by trade) and he grew up in a large, secure family. Like Erasmus he was educated at a school run by the Brethren of the Common Life. He went on to university and, again like Erasmus, he joined the Augustinian Order as a young man – though in his case entirely voluntarily.

Luther is often described as a monk, but more accurately he was what was called a regular canon. He was a member of the order of Augustinian canons which ran hospitals, retirement homes and hospices, and taught in schools and universities. The order had become particularly popular with those who wished to be of some practical service to their fellows, rather than retreat to "the paradise of the cloister". At the end of the tenth chapter of his gospel, Luke tells a story about Jesus visiting two sisters, Martha and Mary, and how, while Mary sat at Jesus's feet to hear what he had to say, Martha "was cumbered about much serving". There is a sense in which the Augustinians were Martha to the Benedictine Mary.

Luther took naturally to the communal life. Prayer, singing and the study of the scriptures filled the life of a novice and he engaged in all of them with enthusiasm. He went regularly to confession and performed his penances scrupulously. In 1506, after just over a year in the noviciate and shortly before his twenty-third birthday, he took his lifelong vows. Then in the spring of 1507 he celebrated the eucharist for the first time. When he came to the words "We offer unto thee, the living, the true, the eternal God", he was overcome with terror. "Who am I", he wrote, "that I should lift up mine eyes or raise my hands to the divine Majesty?" How, he felt, could he presume to address God? The sense of his own unworthiness and sinfulness led him to fear that he was doomed to eternal damnation. He feared the vengeance of God and he asked himself the question *Wie krieg' ich einen barmherzigen Gott?* ("How can I find a merciful God?") Finding a solution to that problem was to dominate his life and influence the course of European history.

As a young man Luther was sent to study theology, and when his order undertook the staffing of the new university of Wittenberg, he became a lecturer there. A few years later he was appointed to be the professor of biblical studies. Later in life he looked back to a time when he was reading Paul's letter to the Romans and was overwhelmed by the importance of the assertion in the twenty-eighth verse of the third chapter that "a man is justified by faith". He saw that as a key thought of immense significance. God could not be placated by good works, by burnt offerings, by payments, penances, pilgrimages or any other human acts. Rather, He offered salvation to those who had faith in him – that is, to those who trusted Him. It seemed clear to Luther that this view of things was to be found in the letters of Paul, in the writings of Augustine of Hippo, and in the mainstream of Christian teaching down the ages. Somehow the church had strayed away from that central aspect of early Christian teaching. He rediscovered it.

Luther was so overwhelmed by Paul's assertion that a man is saved by faith and not by how far he has obeyed the Law, that it led him to dismiss the epistle of James as "an epistle of straw". To Luther it looked as if James was teaching that salvation was by good works, while Paul had understood that it was faith that mattered. But James had been concerned to emphasise that the outcome of faith should be good works. He had in no way disagreed with the teaching of Paul. They both understood that it was more important to understand the teaching of Jesus than to try to define it. They both understood that love is more important than meticulous adherence to rules. They both knew that true faith in Jesus needed to issue in living a good life.

Luther, however, was so concerned to teach that salvation could not be bought by such things as going on pilgrimages, doing penance and buying indulgences, and so confident was he in his opposition to what he thought of as mechanical religion, that he missed the point which the apostle James had been at such pains to emphasize: that faith is worthless if it does not result in conversion of life. Of course, no man could buy salvation by doing good works, but good works are the fruit of faith, and a faith which does not issue in good works is worthless.

It was in the light of his conviction that salvation is by faith that Luther faced the problems raised by the sale of what were known as indulgences. The church had adopted the teaching of Thomas Aquinas that those whose ultimate destination was heaven would first spend some time in the staging-post of purgatory, where they would suffer punishment for their sins. But now it was also teaching that the church could reduce that punishment because of the *plenitudo potestatis*, the "fullness of power", of the pope.

If the pope had full power, why should he not, thought some at the papal curia, use it to free repentant sinners from the pains of purgatory and at the same time turn it into a valuable source of income? Come to that, why should remission from the pains of purgatory be confined to the living? If the pope had the power of God at his disposal, then surely his representatives could give Christians who were prepared to pay the going rate a reduction in the number of years to be spent in purgatory, not only for themselves but also for relations who had died. In the event the papacy turned the sale of indulgences into a money-making racket, and what were called pardoners were sent all round Europe selling indulgences. "As soon as the coin in the coffer rings, the soul straight up to Heaven springs", they proclaimed.

In 1513 a twenty-three-year-old German prince, Albert von Brandenburg, who was trying to establish a dominant position among the other German princes, had himself made both Archbishop of Magdeburg and Bishop of Halberstadt, and the following year he had himself elected Archbishop of Mainz and primate of all Germany as well. By ecclesiastical law he was too young to hold even one bishopric, and holding three involved the sin of pluralism on a significant scale. But Pope Leo X agreed to accept a large sum of money to allow him to do it, and Albert then borrowed the money from the great banking house of Fugger in Augsburg in order to pay the pope.

The next step was to repay the Fuggers, and the pope agreed that Albert could do that by selling indulgences in his territories, keeping half for himself to pay off his debt, and giving the other half to the papacy to go towards the cost of the rebuilding of the magnificent church of St Peter's in Rome. Some of Albert's lands were near Wittenberg, where Luther, now thirty-four years old, was the professor of biblical studies.

Luther saw this sale of indulgences as a disgrace. Not only was it theologically unsound. It also involved moral blackmail of the worst sort. So it was at this point, on 31 October 1517, a date which is widely seen as the beginning of the Protestant Reformation, that he fixed ninety-five theses, "propositions for debate concerned with the question of indulgences", to the door of the castle church in Wittenberg, and announced that he was ready to defend his position in public disputation. If salvation was by faith, as Paul had believed and written, then it did not make sense for it to be traded for cash. When this was reported at Rome, Pope Leo X thought it a relatively trivial matter and told the head of the Augustinian Order to keep Luther quiet.

The consequence was that the argument ceased to be primarily about indulgences and came to be a conflict about the power of the papacy. When Luther was instructed by a papal legate to retract his arguments against indulgences, he refused. If he was to continue to oppose indulgences, he had to deny the authority of the pope. Then, if the pope would not act in accordance with the clear word of God, Luther decided, the ordinary people of Christendom, those whom Peter had described as a "holy priesthood of all believers", would need to rely on the various lay powers, worthy and godly princes, to defend what was right.

In 1520 the papacy issued a bull (a document with the papal seal attached) condemning Luther's propositions as heretical. Luther reacted by burning the papal bull publicly. The following year he was excommunicated, and when asked to recant replied, "Unless I am proved wrong by scripture or by evident reason, then I am a prisoner in conscience to the word of God. I cannot retract and I will not retract. To go against conscience is neither safe nor right. God help me. Amen".

He now began to translate the New Testament into German so that everyone in Germany could know it, and in many states and cities of Germany, especially in the north, the rulers supported reform. A German Bible was placed in church pulpits, services were conducted with the Word of God read in the common tongue, and eventually the singing of Lutheran hymns was included in that worship. Priests were allowed to marry (Luther did) and they began to preach sermons in church, explaining the significance of those passages in the Bible which had been read aloud earlier in the service.

Luther did not see himself as founding a new church. He had no wish to change anything other than that which needed to be reformed, and he did not want to see a split in the church. But he did want the whole church to join in the process of reform. Like Erasmus he preferred reform to having a Reformation. But unlike Erasmus, in the last resort he would stand and fight. Also unlike Erasmus, who had turned away from theology, seeing it as leading to the imposition of uniformity and to persecution, Luther was determined to develop an alternative and sound theology, and was confident that his central belief, the doctrine of salvation by faith, was firmly rooted in the teaching of Paul.

He was sure that it was only on a basis of sound theology that one could hope to build a truly Christian society. Faith had to come first, and salvation was by faith alone. The word "alone" was his own addition, intended to make entirely clear what he believed Paul to have taught. The problem with this was that it led to conflict. He was defying the pope, and meanwhile the papacy for far too long obstinately refused to accept the need for reform. By the time it did, serious and lasting damage had been done. The church was divided, and the divisions generated in the sixteenth century have lasted ever since.

At the time reasonable men on both sides looked for compromise. Cardinal Contarini, who was sympathetic to Luther's teaching on justification by faith, met with the Lutheran layman Philip Melanchthon for a series of talks in 1538–41, and they found that there was much on which they agreed. In the 1560s the Catholic humanist George Cassander expressed clearly and beautifully an ideal for reconciliation: "In essentials, unity; in inessentials, liberty; in everything, charity". It was very much in line with the hopes of Erasmus, who above all wanted goodwill, with a minimum of theology, so that Christians would tolerate differences of opinion. But by then it was too late.

The papacy would not give ground to a rebellious Augustinian, and Luther would not budge either. After all, Paul really does tell us that salvation is by faith, and that was apparent to anyone reading one of the new German Bibles. Luther's clear and simple message swept north Germany and Scandinavia. Many Christians rejoiced to know that salvation comes from faith in God and not from conforming to the requirements of the Church. It was not a matter of believing in the doctrine of salvation by faith. It was a matter of living a life of faith, trusting and following the teaching and example of the Lord Jesus. Thus a Catholic peasant who believes what Protestants may see as superstitious nonsense, but trusts in the forgiving and saving power of Christ, may well be nearer to the Kingdom of Heaven than a Lutheran theologian devoting himself to scholarly definitions of "salvation" and "faith".

Luther was in many ways conservative, but he was above all concerned with the authenticity of individual experience and was opposed to going through the motions of worship without any real feeling. He is sometimes portrayed as opposed to images in worship, and later many of his followers did destroy paintings, statues and stained glass windows, seeing them as false gods. But that was never Luther's intention. He did not believe that his fellow Christians who were Catholics saw images such as crucifixes as objects to be worshipped, and he said so unequivocally: "I believe that there is no person, or certainly very few, who does not understand that the crucifix which stands over there is not my God, for God is in heaven, but rather only a sign".

The trouble with many who followed later and saw themselves as reformers was that they could not distinguish between a sign and that which it signified. Instead of a wooden crucifix or a statue being seen as an aid to worship, it was seen as a wooden or stone object which was worshipped idolatrously and therefore needed to be smashed.

In the twenty-first century there is little or no difference between the Roman and Lutheran churches about the issue of whether salvation is by Faith or by Works, and it is one of Luther's greatest achievements that in the long run he caused the Roman church to undertake its own reformation. Sadly, Roman Catholics and Lutherans remain divided over the issue of authority. For a Roman Catholic authority on matters concerning morals and the Christian faith lies ultimately with the pope, whom they see not only as the successor of the apostle Peter, to whom Jesus had said that he was the rock on which he would build his church, but also as God's representative on Earth. For Lutherans authority lies in the first place with the Bible, and then, when there are disagreements about the Bible's message, it lies with a person's own conscience.

Once the breach had happened there was scope for further disagreement on other issues. Luther's intellectual background was as a Nominalist, so it is no surprise that he rejected the Roman doctrine of transubstantiation, but he made as little change as possible, teaching what came to be known to generations of Lutherans as the doctrine of the real presence. That is, Lutherans were taught to believe that, although the bread and wine remained bread and wine when consecrated, by a divine mystery God was "really" present in the consecrated elements. When the Swiss reformer Ulrich Zwingli taught that those elements were *nuda signa*, "bare signs", acting as a memorial of Jesus, Luther declared that he would "rather drink pure blood with the pope than mere wine with the fanatics".

One important contribution of Luther to Christian thinking took more than four and a half centuries to be appreciated. As early as what is known as the "Heidelberg Disputation" of 1518, six months after the publication of the ninety-five theses against indulgences, Luther publicly criticised what he called the "theology of glory", which emphasised the majesty, might and wisdom of God. In its place he proclaimed the *theologia crucis*, or "theology of the cross", in which he saw God as hidden in the suffering and humiliation of Jesus on the cross. He appreciated Paul's words near the end of his letter to the Christians of Galatia: "God forbid that I should boast of anything but the cross of our Lord Jesus Christ", and his writings make it clear that he believed that the only way to have any knowledge of God was by considering the suffering and death of Jesus. God, who is so effectively hidden from mankind, could not be known, he believed, in any other way.

Luther's *theologia crucis* was not seen as especially important in the sixteenth century and was largely forgotten. It was only with the publication in 1974 of *The Crucified God* by the German theologian Jürgen Moltmann that it came to be appreciated. Not till then did it become clear that Luther's theology centred on the crucified Jesus, whom he saw as the historical manifestation of the faithfulness of God.

Back in the sixteenth century what made Luther so successful was first of all that it seemed obvious to most people, once they thought about it, that he was right to condemn the sale of indulgences. Secondly, he preached the mercy and healing power of God in a manner which anyone could understand. Thirdly, he combined simplicity with a gift for using the German language powerfully. One way in which he spread the faith was by hymns, and the most famous of those hymns was based on psalm 46, which, in the English of Miles Coverdale's translation used in *The Book of Common Prayer*, begins "God is our hope and strength, a very present help in trouble". The first line of

Luther's hymn in German is *Ein feste Burg ist unser Gott, ein gute Wehr und Waffe*, which is usually translated into English as "A safe stronghold our God is still, a trusty shield and weapon".

That was the essence of Luther's message. We must have faith in God, and that is not a matter of giving assent to the proposition that God exists. To Luther it was a matter of trusting God and living a life which reflected that trust. Famously he wrote, "Everything depends on faith. The person who does not have faith is like someone who has to cross the sea, but is so frightened that he does not trust the ship. And so he stays where he is and is never saved". Faith, to Luther, was not a matter of believing that the ship existed. It was a matter of getting aboard in the assurance that it would carry you safely on your journey, and on that journey Christians needed to recognise the transitory nature of the things of this world by comparison with the kingdom of Heaven, which is a spiritual kingdom ruled over by a God who is the creator of all things and inhabits eternity.

When Luther wrote *Ein feste Burg* he was a married man with children, a home and a growing reputation, and he valued all of them. Yet he ends this, his greatest hymn, with the words, "And though they take our life, goods, honour, children, wife, yet is their profit small. These things shall vanish all. The City of God remaineth!" It is much the same message as that taught by Augustine of Hippo more than a thousand years earlier.

Luther died in 1546, nearly a year before the death of King Henry VIII of England, who had broken with Rome for an entirely different reason. By then Lutheran churches were well established in northern Europe. The Scandinavian kingdoms and most of north Germany had broken away from the ecclesiastical jurisdiction of Rome. It is a breach which has never been mended.

Chapter 9

Calvinism, Methodism and the Great Awakening

The English Church, the *ecclesia Anglicana*, eventually known as the Church of England, was by the middle of the sixteenth century neither Roman Catholic nor Lutheran. The English king from 1509 until 1547, Henry VIII, saw himself as a good Catholic, appointed by God to rule the English kingdom. He asserted that authority over the church as well as over the lay state, and he dissolved the monasteries and sold off their vast lands. It is sometimes assumed that the Church of England sought in the sixteenth century to tread a *via media*, a middle way, in ecclesiastical affairs between Roman Catholicism and Lutheranism. Not so. The middle way which some did indeed seek to tread was between Lutheranism and what is often called Calvinism.

John Calvin, who was born in 1509, when Erasmus was in his forties and Luther in his mid-twenties, was just as important a figure in the Protestant Reformation as either of them, and possibly even more influential. He was the son of the business manager for the bishop and cathedral clergy of Noyon in France, and grew up, he later claimed, "obstinately devoted to the superstitions of popery". At the age of fourteen he went to university in Paris to study theology, and after that he studied law.

Then, in his mid-twenties, he experienced a sudden conversion. He felt dominated, or subdued, by God, and for the rest of his life everything he wrote was marked by a continuing consciousness of the absolute sovereignty of God. Characteristically he never told the story of how his conversion happened. He felt called to preach about his Lord and Saviour,

Jesus Christ – not to comment on his own experiences. It was also characteristic of him that he objected to the use of the term "Calvinist", preferring "Reformed", and before he died, at the relatively young age of fifty-five, he gave orders for his burial to be in an unmarked grave.

After an early intellectual diet of theology and law, he set himself to study Hebrew and the writings of the fathers of the early church, especially Augustine of Hippo, and he was still not quite twenty-eight when, in the summer of 1535, a year before Erasmus died and eleven years before the death of Luther, he produced the first version of a book, *The Institutes of the Christian Religion*, which set out his vision of a "Reformed" church and had a dramatic effect on the development of the Reformation. Previous reformers, including Luther, had wanted a moral reformation of the church. They did not want to destroy it and replace it with something else. Calvin did.

The theological underpinning of Calvin's church was above all the idea of the absolute sovereignty of God. Augustine, more than a thousand years earlier, had emphasised the idea of divine grace, and it had led him to consider the possibility of divine foreknowledge of everything. Calvin followed Augustine's thinking to what appeared to him to be its logical conclusion, and that led him to the doctrine of double predestination – the belief that if God had chosen some to be the elect, it followed that he must have destined the others to damnation, and that there was nothing anyone could do about it. One might have expected that to have led to defeatism, but in the sixteenth century it very widely had the opposite effect, as men strove to assure themselves that they were among the elect by doing those good works which they knew were the fruit of faith.

After Calvin's belief in the absolute authority of God, the second essential characteristic of his thinking was his appeal to the authority of scripture. It was to the scriptures that he went, and in particular to the Acts of the Apostles, for guidance on how to construct a church which conformed to the practices of the early church. He also had an extraordinary talent for organisation. These three things, Calvin's belief in the absolute sovereignty of God, his belief in the authority of scripture, and his organising genius, were what between them produced the "reformed" church.

It was, and was intended to be, something entirely new. No longer would there be a church ruled by bishops and priests and presided over, in the case of the Roman Catholics, by the pope and, in the case of the Lutherans, by worthy and godly princes, ruling by divine right in their own territories. Instead, elders chosen from among the holy priesthood of all believers would approve the appointment of godly ministers, or presbyters, who had first been chosen by other pastors. There would be schoolmasters, appointed to ensure the religious training of children, and deacons, appointed to arrange for the care of the sick and the poor. A consistory made up of elders and presbyters would require everyone's regular attendance at church, conformity of belief and moral behaviour. Excommunication would be used to enforce holiness.

Not long afterwards Calvin was able to put his ideas into practice in Geneva, where the city council had thrown out their bishop and were looking for an alternative. What was thereafter practised in Geneva influenced much of Europe, and in particular those areas where there was neither a ruler loyal to Rome nor a godly prince presiding over a Lutheran church. Several of the Swiss cantons adopted the theology and practices of the reformed church, as did some of the multifarious German states, and eventually both the Netherlands and Scotland.

Calvin proclaimed Jesus as prophet, priest and king – a prophet teaching with divine wisdom and authority, a priest offering his own death on the cross as a satisfaction for the sins of all mankind, and the king of a heavenly, or spiritual, kingdom, ruling those who followed him through the work of the Holy Spirit. Calvin's ideas were particularly influential in France, where, early in the second half of the sixteenth century, his followers came to be known as Huguenots. The origin of the word "Huguenot" is unknown, but it appears to have had something to do with their practice of meeting for worship in private houses. Early in the 1560s there were already two million of them in France, and an edict of 1562 gave them permission to practice their religion in their own way, but at the same time imposed restrictions on them, such as not allowing them to bear arms.

Conflict between Catholics and Huguenots became endemic, and a decade of intermittent violence culminated in the Massacre of St Bartholomew's Day, on 23 August 1572, when about forty thousand Huguenots, including many of their leaders, were slaughtered across France by Roman Catholics. It led to the emigration of many of the Huguenots who had survived to England, the Netherlands and various German states, particularly in the north.

It also led to further violence and then civil war in France for a quarter of a century. The warfare was ended in 1598 by the Edict of Nantes, with the Huguenots now tolerated within an officially Catholic France. In theory that toleration lasted until 1685, when the Edict was revoked. In practice it was eroded long before that, and one consequence was the widespread emigration of Huguenots through the world in their tens, even hundreds, of thousands, taking their belief in a reformed church as far as America, South Africa and Australia.

Meanwhile Calvinism had become the established religion of the Netherlands and of Scotland, where it was known as Presbyterianism, and Calvin's ideas were also influential among reformers in England, though never enough for Presbyterianism to become the established church. Calvin's ideas and those of Luther both had a considerable impact in England, but in different ways. Hence the idea that the Church of England was trying to find a *via media* between Lutheranism and Calvinism, which were in some ways as different from each other as they were from Roman Catholicism.

Both accepted the authority of scripture far more than Roman Catholics, for whom the authority of the pope trumped the Bible. But while Luther believed that we should believe and do nothing contrary to scripture, Calvin's view was that in matters of theology and ecclesiastical governance we should believe and do nothing other than that which could be found in or derived from scripture.

In 1559, when he was fifty, Calvin produced the final version of *The Institutes of the Christian Religion*, which became effectively the textbook of his theology and church organisation. He was not a fundamentalist or literalist, so that when, for example, he noticed that Matthew, in the second chapter of his gospel, said, "Then was fulfilled that which was spoken by Jeremiah the prophet", he had no hesitation in pointing out that "it is an obvious mistake to put Jeremiah for Zechariah, for we do not find this saying or anything like it in Jeremiah".

But his whole approach, both to theology and to church organisation, was based on seeking a true understanding of the scriptures, and the essence of his quarrel with Rome was not the corruption or moral laxity of pope and cardinals, but rather that they had removed Jesus from the central place where he so clearly stands in the New Testament. He pointed out that they called on the saints to intercede with God, when Jesus was the one true mediator between Man and God, that they adored the Virgin Mary when only Christ should be adored, and that they had set up a human church which bore little resemblance to the early church described in the Acts of the Apostles.

Calvin's theology, in particular his commitment to the authority of scripture, and also the organisational structure which he devised, divided his reformed church not only from Rome but also from the Lutherans. Luther had rebelled against papal authority and proclaimed his faith in a merciful God. Calvin rebelled against both Catholicism and Lutheranism and presented men with a clear picture of an awful and terrifying God who had to be obeyed.

One area of theology in which Calvin differed significantly from both Rome and Luther was over what takes place at the eucharist. The Roman church still taught the doctrine known as transubstantiation, and at the Council of Trent, which met in some of the years from 1545 to 1563, it was asserted formally that when bread and wine are consecrated by a priest, their substance changes *veriter, realiter, substantialiter*, "really, truly and substantially", into the actual flesh and blood of Jesus. Luther, who had died in 1546, shortly after the Council of Trent first convened, had never been able to accept transubstantiation, but he nevertheless believed in the "real presence" of God in the sacraments, and that belief became an enduring characteristic of the Lutheran church.

Calvin disagreed with both transubstantiation and the idea of "real presence", and instead saw the bread and the wine as "certain, sure and effective signs" of that which they signified. To Calvin God is not present in the bread and wine in any "real" or "corporal" sense, but the sacraments are "effective" in the sense that they have an effect. They point to Christ here and now, not there and then. And the symbolism is important. The bread is manna in our wilderness. It is the bread of life, both literally and metaphorically. And when we drink the wine, he believed, we should remember that Jesus described himself as the true vine.

Much of Calvin's historical importance, however, lies not so much in his theology as in his creation of a new and effective system of church organisation, with elders, presbyters, schoolmasters and deacons. If you want wisdom, go for Erasmus. If you want inspiration, go for Luther. But if you want organisation, then Calvin is your man. In the system known as

Presbyterianism the presbyters were required to be active in both preaching and pastoral care, and together with the elders they regulated the religious life of the community.

While Calvin was a pastor in Geneva, the elders issued regulations about clothing and hairdressing, banned dancing and gambling, and required compulsory attendance at sermons. They knew personally those members of the congregation who were in trouble and those who were troublesome, and they would take action against the ungodly. In a typical year in the 1560s, in a population of 25,000, one person in every fifty was excommunicated for offences against the regulations. Those who were excommunicated were now outside the congregation of the godly, shunned by fellow Christians and threatened with eternal damnation until they repented and mended their wicked ways.

While Luther had set out to remedy corruption, Calvin set out to enforce holiness. The elect had to keep themselves pure and unspotted from the world and prove both to themselves and to others that they were saved. The clarity of Calvin's theology and the efficiency of his organisational structure provided men with the certainty which many of them wanted, and for the next hundred years or so Calvinism was the most powerful force in Protestantism. Where it took root, it took over. While Luther secularized the church, Calvin clericalized the state.

Wherever there was Presbyterian church government there was also Calvinist doctrine, and the disciplinary bodies of the Calvinist churches would take action just as much against someone who held the Lutheran doctrine of the real presence as they would against someone who held the Catholic doctrine of transubstantiation. Both beliefs were seen by the Calvinists as vain superstition. Similarly, the Calvinists would sing neither the Latin chants of the Roman Catholics nor Lutheran hymns, on the grounds that they were not scriptural, and they came to be renowned for their renderings of the metrical versions of the psalms.

Whereas the translations of the psalms by Miles Coverdale, which are to be found in the Anglican *Book of Common Prayer* have neither a regular rhythm nor a rhyme scheme, the metrical versions authorised by the Presbyterian Church of Scotland have both. For example, the Coverdale version of psalm 100, the *Jubilate Deo*, begins, "O be joyful in the Lord, all ye lands; serve the Lord with gladness, and come before his presence with a song", while the Scottish metrical version begins, "All people that on earth do dwell, Sing to the Lord with cheerful voice; Him serve with fear, his praise forth tell, Come ye before him, and rejoice". It is worth noticing not only the rhythm and rhyme scheme, but also that the one significant addition is the words, "Him serve with fear". That shows the influence of Calvinist theology. It was entirely acceptable to Presbyterian congregations in the sixteenth and seventeenth centuries, and possibly still is today.

The metrical versions of the psalms became entrenched in the Scottish consciousness. As late as 1931, when the Labour Party in Great Britain was overwhelmingly defeated in a general election, but four Labour candidates nevertheless won the four seats in central Glasgow, their supporters accompanied them to the station, triumphantly singing not *The Red Flag* or *The Internationale* but metrical versions of the psalms.

In Scotland, as in Holland, Calvin's teaching on salvation gave hope of salvation for centuries to many thousands of those who followed it. Calvinists, or Presbyterians, saw themselves as men and women of faith, called by God's grace, through no merit of their own, to read the scriptures and wrestle with the Lord in prayer, always seeking to do those good works which were the fruit of their salvation and also a sign that the Lord would not allow them to fall away.

In the last resort, Calvin believed, God's choice of the elect and the damned was known only to Him. But a good life on Earth strongly suggested election and many Calvinists struggled to demonstrate their own salvation to themselves. Eventually many saw material success in this world, achieved by working hard and conscientiously, as God's blessing on those who were honest, sober, thrifty and hard-working – a sort of Protestant sacrament, in which the outward and visible sign of material success in this world pointed to the inward invisible grace of God awaiting them in the next.

It is not a view Calvin would have recognised. Quite the contrary, he even suggested, when writing a commentary on the prophet Hosea, that one should not rejoice at prosperity, but rather see it as a possible occasion for God's anger. Nevertheless, the idea of prosperity as a sign of God's favour took hold, and it is still widely accepted in the twenty-first century.

By the 1530s Europe was divided into Roman Catholic, Lutheran and Calvinist areas. England was in none of those camps. Its king, Henry VIII, asserted his authority as a king ordained by God, with the right and the duty to control the Catholic church in his own kingdom. He repudiated both the authority of the pope in Rome and the teaching of Martin Luther. At one time he had two Roman Catholic priests hanged, drawn and quartered, since that was the appropriate punishment for treason, while he had two Lutheran ministers burnt to death, since that was the way he dealt with heresy.

During the reign of his son, Edward VI, from 1547 until 1553, when discussion was free and no one was condemned as a heretic, Calvinist reformers arrived in England from the continent and some of the clergy of the Church of England adopted aspects of Calvinist theology. Then Edward's successor and half-sister, Queen Mary, imposed Roman Catholicism vigorously, persecuting Protestants and burning Anglican bishops to death. After her death in 1558, Henry VIII's other daughter, Queen Elizabeth, tried to establish religion much as it had been towards the end of her father's reign.

Elizabeth wanted a national church acceptable to all. It was not possible. The divisions had gone too deep, and although she tried to tread the middle road, or *via media*, between Lutheranism and Calvinism, by the end of the century the religious divisions in the country were bitter and the civil wars of the next century were as much about religion as about the constitution. England was a country in which Calvinist theology was widespread, but it was without a Presbyterian system of church government, because the established church remained the Church of England, with its bishops and parish clergy. Those Calvinists who felt that they could not accept this had to find a way of operating as separate, or independent, congregations, each electing its own minister. In the seventeenth century they were known as Independents. By the eighteenth century they were more commonly known as Congregationalists.

The continent went through comparable upheavals, with the Wars of Religion in France and a Thirty Years War in Germany, and to many people it seemed as if civilization was collapsing. But as happens so often in human affairs, what looked like an ending turned out with hindsight to have been the beginning of something new. Both on the continent and in England the idea of toleration emerged, not because anyone believed in it as an ideal, but because the only way to bring the killing to an end was to agree to live side by side with those with whom one disagreed.

Much else was changing, and eventually one of the most significant changes was in where people lived. Large towns were developing and people were moving from the countryside to work in them. But the parish system in England remained largely unchanged. Thus there came to be many small villages in the countryside with a declining population, where a clergyman, usually a member of the upper classes, lived in a large vicarage with a substantial income from his benefice, perhaps paying a curate a low stipend to care for the relatively small number of people in the parish, while at the same time towns such as Manchester and Birmingham were growing vastly in size but had no more provision for the care of their populations than they had had in the past. The Church of England seriously neglected the care of the people in those towns.

Meanwhile in Europe the Protestant Reformation had shifted assumptions in the direction of expecting personal commitment from each believer, and for many this had led to the belief that Christianity should be about transforming lives rather than about theological correctness. In the Lutheran territories of northern Europe people who came to be known as Pietists would attend normal services, but would also meet in private houses to study the Bible, pray, and join each other in good works. As Lutherans they knew that salvation was "by faith alone", but they also knew that their faith had to lead on to good works. Pietism became a shining example of reform at work.

England eventually produced its own brand of Pietism when an energetic clergyman, John Wesley, who lived from 1703 until 1791, went round urban areas, those which had a growing population but no church, preaching and attracting large crowds. As a young man he had been impressed by the way the Pietists stressed the need for a living faith, shunned theology, responded emotionally to Christ as their Lord and Saviour, and sought a personal relationship with him.

Another influence on him was the teaching of a Dutch theologian, Jakob Hermanszoon, better known by the Latinized version of his name, Jacobus Arminius, who in the late sixteenth century had reacted against the Calvinist doctrine of double predestination and asserted that Christ had died for all mankind, not only for the elect, and that anyone could be saved who believed in Jesus as the Christ, persevered in that faith and followed him obediently. It was a sermon preached in

London by an Arminian Pietist missionary in May 1738 which, said Wesley, warmed his heart and led him thereafter to teach that the spirit of God can reach any open heart and transform a person's life.

His theology was dramatically different from that of John Calvin in that he was moved by the assertion in the fourth verse of the second chapter of Paul's first letter to Timothy that "God willeth all men to be saved". To John Wesley it seemed that everyone could be saved by faith in Jesus Christ. He believed, and taught, that "fulfilment of the law of Christ" was a matter of living with regard for others and their welfare.

Throughout England he found people eager to hear him preach a gospel of hope and willing to follow his demand that they should live lives with some method in them. What he expected of those who came to "Methodist" meetings was that they should obey three rules, which, in brief, were these: do no harm; do as much good as you can; and use all the means of grace that God has provided.

His reaction against Calvinism took him as far as seeing the possibility of salvation for those of other religions. He still believed that the full assurance of salvation was only possible through a relationship with Christ, but he shifted away from the traditional exclusiveness of Christianity to an assertion that anyone, of whatever nation or religion, who feared God and behaved righteously was acceptable to God. His attitude can be seen as a first step towards the ecumenical and inter-faith approach which would become increasingly popular with many Christians in the twentieth century.

Something which Wesley had in common with Calvin was a genius for organisation. He saw the need, if the movement he had started was to flourish, both for a system of communication and for accountability, and he developed what he called a "connection". He arranged annual conferences of both lay leaders and clergy, at which it was hoped that God's will would be revealed to them. He developed a vast network of lay preachers, including women, and he devised the idea of ensuring that preaching remained vigorous, and that congregations should have something new to hear, by instituting "circuits", with preachers having to move from one congregation to another every year or two.

Methodism flourished with its preaching, with visits to people's houses, and with the singing of hymns, many of the best of them written by John Wesley's brother, Charles. Some of those hymns can be heard today sung by Anglican and Roman Catholic congregations, and the opening lines of the best known of them indicate both the tone of Methodism and what was characteristic about Wesley's theology. One begins "Love Divine, all loves excelling". The opening of another is "Amazing love! How can it be that thou, my God, should die for me?" Yet another begins "Jesu, Lover of my soul, Let me to thy bosom fly", and another, "Love's redeeming work is done". The tone is entirely different from dour, Scottish Presbyterianism. It captivated thousands.

John Wesley remained an Anglican clergyman, insisting that he would "live and die a member of the Church of England", and he did. But the hierarchy of the established church failed to take advantage of him or of the movement he had started. He wanted some of his lay preachers to be ordained, especially to meet the growing demand for ministers in the American colonies, but he met the obstacle that the Church of England was committed to the idea of apostolic succession. That is, there was a belief that every bishop had been consecrated by other bishops in an unbroken line going back to the early apostles, and that all clergy needed to be ordained by those bishops.

Ideally that problem would have been resolved by making Wesley a bishop, but at the time he did not fit the image of an Anglican bishop, any more than his ministers fitted the image of Anglican clergy, and the opportunity was missed. In 1784, after many years of frustration, and the year after the American War of Independence ended, he took it upon himself to ordain ministers to serve the ever-growing Methodist congregations in America. A breach with the hierarchy of the Church of England became inevitable and after his death in 1791 a new denomination of Methodism came into existence.

Back in the 1740s, as Methodism was developing in England, similar ideas were spreading through North America. Many early settlers there had been Calvinists, both Presbyterians and Congregationalists, but other denominations were also able to establish themselves, and as new immigrants opened up the West, it was particularly the Baptists and the Methodists who flourished. As the population grew and new immigrants set off westwards to find land for themselves and farm it, there was at first little or no organized religion in the new lands. Life was hard, and in the early eighteenth century religion appeared to be in decline. But then in the 1740s there came what is known as the Great Awakening, a religious revival spread by word of mouth, which was little to do with doctrine but much to do with living a simple and holy life.

A Congregationalist minister in Massachusetts, Jonathan Edwards, who was born in 1703, the same year as John Wesley, was renowned in his own time for his impressive and influential preaching. He has a lasting importance because of his work as a theologian who, like Arminius before him, and despite being a Congregationalist, rebelled against Calvin's belief in double predestination. He shifted the emphasis in his sermons from God's anger towards sinful men to the idea that God's love radiated such goodness and beauty that even "persons of mean capabilities and advantages" could love beauty in all its varied forms and, loving beauty, could worship the God of Love.

He wrote memorably of his "sheer beholding" of God's beauty. "As I was walking there and looking up into the sky and the clouds, there came into my mind so sweet a sense of the majesty and grace of God, that I know not how to express them both in sweet conjunction". That is, he saw the majesty of God as something gracious rather than tyrannical, and at the same time he saw the grace of God as something majestic. His writings also show a clear belief that theological understanding must go hand in hand with pastoral care. Not surprisingly his sermons were printed and widely disseminated.

Meanwhile Wesley's ideas had crossed the Atlantic and numerous preachers were telling their congregations that God's saving grace was open to all. The combination of the ideas of Wesley and Jonathan Edwards had the effect that the distinctions between one Protestant denomination and another came to be blurred. Whether a preacher was Presbyterian, Congregationalist, Methodist or Baptist, he would be calling on his congregation to be "converted" and "new born" to a life in Christ. Increasingly those preachers were Methodists and Baptists.

The principal theological idea that had for generations distinguished the Baptists was that a person had to "come to faith" as an adult before being baptised. The distinctive theological position of the Methodists was that God offered salvation to all, but it was up to each individual to accept it. These ideas combined as Americans pushed westwards, and there were recurrent bursts of revivalist fervour. The rigidities of Calvinist doctrine were less well suited to this environment than was the fervour of Baptists and Methodist preachers, who, in a wild and violent society, exhorted men to repent, praise the Lord, give thanks for His goodness and the gift of salvation, support their neighbours when in need, and ask for God's blessing and protection.

There was usually little theological content to the preaching, and the emphasis on personal salvation and on the importance of loving God and one's neighbour was accompanied by a neglect of those issues raised in the gospels to do with wealth and poverty and the use and abuse of power. Gradually a society was created in which men and women worshipped their Lord and Saviour and helped their neighbours, while some of them killed native Americans to make way for farms, railways and mines, others exploited black slaves to grow cotton, and most adopted the values of consumerism.

By the time of the American Civil War of 1861–1865 Methodism was the largest single denomination in the USA, but it was divided in four. There were both Northern and Southern Methodists, and the black and white congregations were segregated in the North as well as in the South. The Civil War was precipitated by the attempt of the southern states, whose economy was based on the institution of slavery, to secede from the union, and it ended with those states ruined. Since that time Americans throughout the USA, most of them counting themselves as Christians, have been living with problems inherited from the past, not least the question of how far the descendants of both slaves and native Americans could have equality in what saw itself as a Christian society. Those problems remain difficult to resolve. There were great merits in the personal religion of what came to be known as "the Baptist Bible Belt", but the merits of personal religion did not appear to be able to solve the entrenched problems of American society.

Chapter 10

The Scientific Revolution and the Enlightenment

In Western Europe Christianity emerged from the Middle Ages as an amalgam of ideas derived from the New Testament, the Old Testament, Greek philosophy, and the accumulated thinking of the early fathers of the church and medieval theologians. But it was no longer one united Roman church, proclaiming to the orthodox churches of the east that it was the only true and universal church. Instead, although there were still many Roman Catholics, there were also Lutherans, Calvinists, Anglicans, Baptists and some other smaller sects, all divided from each other above all by the question of who should exercise authority in the church. Bitter conflicts among Christians in the west continued through the sixteenth century and into the seventeenth, culminating in the Thirty Years War, which eventually ended in 1648 with the opposing sides agreeing a measure of toleration, not because either side believed in toleration, but because it was the only way to avoid continuing bloodshed.

On most matters of theology they were united, but not all. As early as the end of the fourteenth century William of Ockham's questioning of the whole system of thought derived from Plato and Aristotle and known to philosophers as Realism had undermined what was taught as the doctrine of transubstantiation. If there was no such thing as "substance", then the doctrine no longer made sense. It also undermined the theoretical underpinning of the idea that Jesus was "of one substance with the Father", but by then the idea that Jesus was one of the three persons of the Trinity was so well established that the early thinking which underpinned it no longer mattered.

The churches of Western Europe very largely retained both the ideas and the liturgy they had inherited from the past, but before long their shared beliefs were to be challenged by new developments in the realm of ideas. The western church had over the centuries lost touch with the more intellectual and metaphorical way of thinking of the East, and in both Catholic and Protestant churches in Western Europe it was entirely usual in the sixteenth century for their members to think in literal terms of heaven as a kingdom high in the sky ruled over by God, and hell as a fiery region beneath the earth ruled by the Devil. So firmly was that way of thinking ingrained in people's minds that the sky was often spoken of as "the heavens".

Strangely enough, that picture of heaven and hell as real places, rather than as metaphorical images to illustrate the difference between good and evil, has its origins in part in the picture of the universe worked out in ancient Greece by Aristotle. Aristotle had seen the earth as a solid, immobile sphere at the centre of the universe. His perception was that the silver orb of the moon moved around the earth in a perfect circle, and somewhat further away the golden orb of the sun moved in another perfect circle. Beyond that was the bowl of the heavens, with the stars moving together in an even grander circle. Up in the heavens everything was perfect. Down on Earth, at the centre of the universe, in the sublunary sphere, the area beneath the moon, was the imperfect Earth. All that was needed for the Christian church to complete the picture was to locate hell under the ground.

That Aristotelian world view fitted extraordinarily well with Christian theology. The idea of an imperfect Earth fitted with the story of the Fall, in which Adam and Eve are driven out of the Garden of Eden, and although Jesus insisted that his kingdom was not of this world but instead was a spiritual kingdom, considering what he had meant by that was a lot more difficult than thinking of heaven as a physical place beyond the stars which was inhabited by angels, and of hell as another place beneath the ground, in this case inhabited by demons.

As universities had developed during the Middle Ages an important element in the curriculum was astronomy, precisely because it was concerned with the heavens, and astronomy threw up a puzzling problem whose solution was to generate what is now thought of as the scientific revolution. That solution was eventually to have an impact on theological ideas as well as on science.

While most stars stay in the same position in relation to each other and seem to move together round the earth in a circular orbit, a few, which we now know as planets, wander around the heavens in what seemed to be a quite irrational fashion. By the end of the fifteenth century, it was clear to a small number of mathematical astronomers that no existing explanation of these "wandering stars" was satisfactory.

One of those mathematical astronomers was a canon of the cathedral of Frauenburg on the shores of the Baltic called Nicolaus Copernicus. When working on this problem he had an extraordinary idea which he published in 1543, by which time he was seventy, in a book called *De Revolutionibus Orbium Caelestium*, or "Concerning the Revolutions of the Heavenly Orbs". It put forward the startling notion that the earth moves in an annual orbit around the sun and at the same time rotates on its axis, which has the effect of producing day and night. Copernicus also argued that not only Earth but the "wandering stars", or planets, were also orbiting the sun.

Common sense was against it. Could one really imagine Earth sweeping through space and revolving as it went? Even mathematical astronomers who were interested in Copernicus's ideas usually avoided considering how they might relate to reality. The implications were too great to be tackled. And it was not only that common sense was against it. It was also that the stars did not appear to move in relation to each other, as one would expect if the earth were swinging vast distances through space. All the stars except the planets seem to stay in the same positions in relation to each other and move as one.

The only way Copernicus could explain this was by postulating a universe so large that the orbit of the earth around the sun was trivial in relation to the stars, which were unbelievably vast distances away. As it happens, we now know that the earth is never much more than about eight light minutes away from the sun, which is trivial in relation to the stars, which are light years away. The planets, however, are part of our own solar system, and, like Earth, are relatively near the sun, so while the stars stay in fixed positions in relation to each other, the planets are seen to wander around the sky.

Just after the start of the seventeenth century the Italian mathematician and physicist Galileo built a telescope and used it to observe the heavens. He described his observations in a book called *The Starry Messenger*, which was published in 1610. First, he claimed that the moon was not perfectly spherical and smooth, but "full of irregularities". It was, he suggested, as imperfect as the earth. Secondly, though a telescope would normally magnify things, stars looked no bigger when observed through a telescope than they did to the naked eye. The only conclusion to be drawn was that the stars were so far away that the claim Copernicus had made that the universe might be almost unbelievably large began to seem more reasonable. Thirdly, Galileo observed and described four satellites orbiting Jupiter. If that was true, then at a stroke it destroyed the idea of a geocentric universe with the earth at its centre and everything else going round it in perfect circular orbits. If there was an exception in the case of Jupiter, the whole structure fell apart.

The implications were disturbing. At the time the cardinals and bishops of the Catholic church in Italy saw themselves and their ideas as being under threat from the Protestant Reformation in northern Europe, and they determined to hold the line on what they saw as an essential Christian belief. In 1616 the inquisition declared that the opinion that the sun was at the centre of the universe was "foolish and absurd, philosophically false and formally heretical". Galileo was arrested and, in fear of torture and death, made his confession, swearing to abandon "the false opinion that the sun is the centre of the world and immovable" as a detestable heresy. It is one of the most striking examples in human history of the temporary nature of the triumph of authority over rational thought. Even as Galileo swore to accept the traditional Aristotelian view, he knew that it was finished.

The disagreement continued into the twentieth century, and it is some measure of its extent that it was not until 1992, three hundred and fifty years after the death of Galileo, that Pope John Paul II officially forgave him. Nor was it a problem only for Catholics. Some fundamentalist Protestants saw the second verse of the ninety-third psalm, "He hath made the round world so sure that it cannot be moved", as a clear refutation of the Copernican system. To them the Bible was just as much against Copernicus and Galileo as was the pope.

But the disagreement was an entirely unnecessary one. Nothing in the Copernican system contradicts the teaching of Jesus. Ideally the church would have recognised that, and the discoveries of scientists would have helped them appreciate what was and what was not important in Christianity. The command of Jesus to his followers that they should love God and also love their neighbour as themselves was important. The question of whether the sun orbited the earth or the earth orbited the sun was fascinating but entirely irrelevant to Christian thinking.

The scientific revolution was, however, to have a profoundly unsettling effect on Christian thinking, as one astronomer after another built on the ideas of Copernicus. Eventually Isaac Newton (1643–1727), born a year after the death of Galileo, not only worked out why the planets move as they do but also, for most practical purposes, solved the problem of how the whole universe operates. In 1687 he published *Philosophiae Naturalis Principia Mathematica*, which can be loosely translated as "The Mathematical Principles which explain how the Universe Works", and in it he set out universally applicable laws of motion.

Not only were traditional ideas about the universe shaken, but many widely accepted ideas about God and heaven were shaken as well, and eventually this affected the view of the relationship between God and Man in history. The picture we see in the early books of the Old Testament of an all-powerful God, the creator of all things, guiding his chosen people and intervening in human affairs to determine the course of history, now had to be questioned.

The next step was a change in understanding of the New Testament story. Traditionally Christians had seen that as an account of a loving God reaching out through his Son to all mankind, and it was widely believed that thereafter God had frequently intervened in human affairs, often in response to prayer, to alter the course of history. But in the late seventeenth century there was a shift towards the view that God, instead of intervening on particular occasions, had set the universe going and was standing back while it continued along its pre-determined course.

The view of William of Ockham that there is a distinction between God's *potentia absoluta*, or absolute power, which existed before the beginning of time, and the *potentia ordinata*, which has existed since creation, had come into its own. Instead of expecting God to intervene in response to prayer, it was now asserted, we should expect Him to be reliable. No amount of prayer would change the weather, prevent an earthquake or stop a war. Nor should one expect it to do so.

Meanwhile, perhaps as a defensive reaction, there was a move, particularly among Protestants, towards a more literal way of interpreting the scriptures. By the eighteenth century the world of the imagination was increasingly viewed by many people with suspicion. Anything mysterious or marvellous which had once been a source of awe and wonder was dismissed as false. Such stories as those in Luke's gospel about the events surrounding the birth of Jesus were no longer accepted as a beautiful proclamation that something wonderful had happened. The idea of an angel appearing in the sky with a multitude of the heavenly host praising God, and saying "Glory to God in the highest, and on Earth peace, goodwill toward men" would be dismissed by many on the grounds that such things simply do not happen in real life. To that Christians often reacted by asserting that such stories were literally true. If they did not themselves feel entirely confident about it themselves, they felt guilty about their own lack of faith.

There was increasingly a demand for the right answer to all moral problems, and while many Catholics expected Holy Church to give them the right answers, many Protestants expected the scriptures to do the same. The world of the spirit had to be defined, and sadly it became a matter of authority – of deciding who was entitled to define the truth. Many Protestants saw themselves as the People of the Book and they treated the words of the Bible as sacrosanct. Thus they felt obliged to believe them and carried that obligation to the point at which, if they encountered something clearly implausible, they would pray, "Lord, I believe. Help Thou my unbelief". They would accuse Roman Catholics of Mariolatry, the worship of Mary, the mother of Jesus, and Roman Catholics replied by accusing them of Bibliolatry, the worship of the Bible.

The great problem which bedevilled Christian thinking was that Christians often wanted all others to have to give assent to what they believed themselves, and if they were in a position to require others to do so, then they imposed that requirement. Roman Catholics claimed to be sure that Holy Church was right and during the Reformation era would burn to death Protestants who did not agree. Some Protestants claimed to be similarly sure that they were right and would burn Catholics to death. Instead of knowing that they were passed from death into life because they loved the brethren, as the apostle John had written (1 John chapter 3 verse 14), Christians were engaged in reciprocal enmity and violence. Evil bred evil.

Meanwhile the shift in the generally accepted view of the nature of the universe, together with a shift in the understanding of God, was followed by a loosening of the constraints of both religion and morality. By the eighteenth century Europe was entering a period which came to be known as the Age of Enlightenment, in which conventional wisdom was challenged. It was not that all the thinkers of the Enlightenment were opposed to Christianity, but rather that the context in which they thought and wrote was no longer an exclusively religious one.

Even before the end of the seventeenth century an English philosopher, John Locke, had produced a rational defence of toleration. Toleration had developed as a practical expedient to avoid continuing bloodshed. Locke now argued that it was intrinsically a good principle which could be defended in three ways. His first contention was that no human being can judge reliably between two differing religious positions. The second was that belief, as distinct from outward conformity, cannot be enforced. The third was that the consequences of seeking to compel conformity will always be worse than permitting diversity.

The exact meaning of the term Age of Enlightenment varies from one country to another, but there is general agreement that it was an eighteenth century European philosophical movement which undermined traditional ideas about monarchy and the church. In France the *Siècle des Lumières* was seen as the period from the death of Louis XIV in 1715 to the outbreak of the French Revolution in 1789. During that time Voltaire (1694–1778) in his novel *Candide* challenged the idea that all is for the best in this best of all possible worlds, and Rousseau (1712–1778) argued that in a state of nature Man, far from being originally sinful, was naturally good, though liable to be corrupted by the chains of tyranny.

In Scotland David Hume (1711–76), while still a young man, had decided that all human knowledge comes through our senses and that it was impossible for the human mind to give meaningful expression to anything beyond what we can tell from our senses. Meanwhile in Germany Immanuel Kant (1724–1804), who is widely thought of as the father of modern philosophy, contended that the source of all morality is Reason.

As the vastness of the universe came to be appreciated it was possible for both Christians and non-Christians to realise that we cannot know all the secrets of the universe, for we are ourselves a part, even if only a very small part, of what we are trying to understand. We cannot possibly stand outside the universe and view it objectively, but we can do our best to try to understand more. The German philosopher Gotthold Lessing (1729–81) famously wrote that if God gave him a choice between all truth and continuing to strive for truth while perpetually making mistakes, he would choose to go on striving and making mistakes. Perfect truth, he said, is for God alone.

Important political developments still found their justification in the Christian tradition. That is so of the opening words of the American Declaration of Independence of 1776: "We hold these truths to be self-evident, that all men are created equal, that they are endowed by their Creator with certain unalienable rights, that among these are Life, Liberty and the pursuit of Happiness". But those words inaugurate the setting up of a constitution in which there was to be no established religion, not because Americans generally were opposed to religion, but because, while many of them cared passionately about it, they could not agree on what form their religion should take.

A few years later there was revolution in France, which not only overthrew the king and the nobility but the church as well. Yet it took place under the slogan "Liberty, Equality and Brotherly Love", all of which were clearly derived from the Christian tradition. But by now the Enlightenment, which had been characterized by the view that Reason should be able to resolve all problems, had run into the problem that "reasonable" men often found it difficult to agree with each other.

Then the Enlightenment was challenged by the Romantic Movement. To the Romantics it seemed possible that the imagination could soar above that which we can perceive with our senses and discern truths which were beyond the scope of Reason. "I am certain of nothing but the holiness of the heart's affections and the truth of the imagination", wrote John Keats (1795–1821), and Robert Browning (1812–1889) wrote, "Ah, but a man's imagination should exceed his grasp, Or what's a heaven for?"

Such sentiments were not necessarily Christian, but they often were. Thus, shortly before the end of his extraordinary and very long poem *The Rime of the Ancient Mariner*, Samuel Taylor Coleridge (1772–1834) puts into the mouth of the ancient mariner the words, "He prayeth best who loveth best all things both great and small, for the dear God who loveth us, He made and loveth all".

But for all the persistence of the Christian tradition, the various ideas of the Enlightenment had seriously shaken traditional Christian ideas. It was now possible to live in European society without any religious belief, and in the second half of the nineteenth century the German philosopher Friedrich Nietzsche (1844–1900) declared that civilization had reached a point at which the idea of God was no longer needed. "God is dead!", he wrote in 1882, and went on to declare that "we", the men of nineteenth century Europe, "have killed him!"

Meanwhile the scientific revolution continued, and every change had some impact on traditional Christian views. In particular, there was a widespread assumption in Europe well into the eighteenth century that all living creatures were descendants of those which had been created by God in the beginning and saved by Noah from dying in a great flood (Genesis 6–8). But early in the nineteenth century that view became untenable as geologists brought people face to face with the fossil evidence of ever-changing variety in a world clearly much older than it would appear to be from a reading of the Book of Genesis.

The study of geology led the way towards the idea of evolution, but it was still possible, and even usual, for Christians to take the view that, although the earth was far older than had previously been thought, the perfectly ordered universe, whose workings had been revealed by the devoutly Christian Sir Isaac Newton, was evidence of "intelligent design" by a beneficent creator, and that that creator had, for example, generously provided all the materials for food and shelter that could be needed by humankind.

In 1859 another Englishman, Charles Darwin (1809–1882), who had devoted his life to understanding how the various different forms of life came into existence, published *On the Origin of Species by Means of Natural Selection*, which revealed a process which did not need the direct intervention of a creator. If an animal could run faster, reach higher or co-operate with others better than most of its fellows, that gave it an advantage which, in particular circumstances, enabled it to survive and breed and thus pass on its distinctive characteristics to its descendants. Thus all living creatures evolved. Some species became extinct. New species came into existence. There was no need for "intelligent design".

Right from the beginning some clergy, such as Charles Kingsley (1819–1875), and many other Christians welcomed this advance in scientific understanding and accepted the readjustment it required to some religious ideas. They still saw the Bible as a divinely inspired collection of illuminating writings, but they no longer interpreted it literally, and they welcomed *On the Origin of Species* for the insight it provided into the nature of the created order. Darwin, they realised, was explaining what happened and even, to some extent, how it happened. He was not commenting on what was right or wrong, and most certainly was not asserting a general principle that it was somehow right that the strong should triumph over the weak. But many Christians feared what they saw as a threat to their established beliefs, and Bishop Samuel Wilberforce of Oxford (1805–1873) was voicing a widely held view when he declared that "the principle of natural selection is absolutely incompatible with the Word of God".

Sadly, Darwin's theory of the origin of species by a process of natural selection came to be confused with a crude idea of "the survival of the fittest", which was widely seen to flow naturally from the theory of "natural selection". A range of developments flowed from this misunderstanding and many conscientious Christians were shocked by them. Some entrepreneurs saw "Darwinism" as a justification for exploiting the poor and weak, while Karl Marx saw it as the biological counterpart to the class struggle and wanted to dedicate the English edition of *Capital* to Darwin, who declined the honour.

The German General Staff of the early twentieth century saw war as a "biological necessity" and believed that the Germans, as the most advanced human race, would defeat all lesser peoples, such as the Latins (e.g., the French) and the Slavs (e.g., the Russians), and by a process of "natural selection" would come to dominate the world. It is widely forgotten nowadays that that extreme and objectionable form of racism, which played so large a part in bringing about the First World War, long predates the rise of Nazism.

The crude idea that "the survival of the fittest" is a matter of the biggest and strongest killing or enslaving the weak understandably turned people against what they mistakenly believed to be Darwin's ideas. What Darwin was teaching was that the bright colours of a flower or of a bird's plumage may make it particularly fit to survive in certain situations, and the capacity of tiny ants to co-operate may enable them to flourish. He could have pointed out that a good survival strategy for young adult male human beings as war threatens is to be physically weak and unfit for military service. Tigers and polar bears are big and strong, but there are a lot more antelopes than tigers and a lot more seals than polar bears, and the tigers die out when their habitat is turned to agriculture, and the polar bears starve as the ice melts.

One area where "Darwinism" was seen as particularly objectionable was in the southern states of the United States. There the post-Enlightenment practice of imposing a literal interpretation on the Bible was widespread, and in the early 1920s several of the southern states passed laws outlawing the teaching of "Darwinism" in their schools. Instead, they wanted their children to be taught "Creationism", which involves a literal interpretation of the Bible, in this case of the first chapter of the Book of Genesis.

It was understandable. It was possible to foresee that a logical extension of what was misguidedly called "Darwinism" could be such things as programmes for eliminating the sick, the old and the weak, and even aiming to breed "superior" human beings who would dominate the rest of mankind. It was not until 1988, by which time the Nazi attempt to do that in Europe was more than forty years in the past, that a judgement of the Supreme Court of the USA declared the imposition of "creation science" in schools to be a violation of the first amendment to the American Constitution, which is an amendment guaranteeing freedom of speech.

Darwin's ideas had shaken conventional Christian assumptions in the nineteenth century as much as Copernicus and Galileo had shaken the assumptions of their day. Some Christians abandoned their faith, but others saw it as a challenge to think again about the significance of the Gospel message and separate what was essential from conventional accretions. Inevitably, some wondered if Christianity was compatible with science. For centuries the Christian churches had made assertions about matters which properly fall into the realm of scientific exploration. While science was in its infancy that did not particularly matter. Once science came of age it mattered a great deal, and at the end of the twentieth century the distinguished American evolutionary biologist Stephen Jay Gould (1941–2002) argued that science and religion should keep to their own areas of competence and not intrude on each other.

Gould's case for separating science and religion is preferable to the attitude of the occasional atheist fundamentalist who seeks to exalt empirical science into the only truth, for in the past "scientific" atheism has led to eugenics programmes and such aberrations as the Nazi attempt to exterminate all Jews or the Bolshevik attempt to exterminate "class enemies". But fortunately, it is not necessary to choose between on the one hand the scrupulous avoidance of any exchange of ideas between religion and science and on the other hand the deification of empirical science as a substitute for religion.

Science is concerned with seeking a fuller understanding of the material world, from the microcosms of sub-atomic particles to the macrocosm of the universe, and scientists are concerned with pushing out the bounds of knowledge. It is in the nature of science that its hypotheses are capable of being disproved. That is what makes them "scientific". Later scientists will develop and modify them, and the Christian church needs to recognise that scientific advances, properly understood, are no threat to the theological, spiritual and moral issues which are the proper concern of the church. They should welcome what scientists have to tell them. Scientists, meanwhile, should avoid assuming any special competence in the fields of religion and moral philosophy. Ideally scientists, theologians and moral philosophers will learn to share their insights with each other, and then they may sometimes find that ideas in one area of thought have value in another.

The leaders of the Christian church made the mistake in the seventeenth century of thinking that a particular and outdated view of how the universe was constructed was essential to Christianity. It was not. Similarly, many leaders of the Christian church made the mistake in the nineteenth century of thinking that a view of creation based on a belief in the literal accuracy of the first chapter of the Book of Genesis was essential to Christianity. It was not. In both cases the advances in scientific understanding should have caused them to reconsider what it is in Christianity that really matters.

Scientific advances should have been an invaluable aid to the Christian church in helping it appreciate which components of widespread Christian belief were really a distraction from what really matters. Instead, the church was usually grudging in its acceptance of scientific advances. It often seemed to want to cling to beliefs and assumptions which had made sense a thousand or more years ago but now needed to be re-thought in the light of what science was able to tell us. But it gave ground reluctantly. Christians need to appreciate that there is every reason why Christianity and the search for greater understanding through science should co-exist happily. Some theologians have been saying that for a long while, but they are seldom heard.

Ideas are powerful things, and whether Darwin's theory of the origin of species is seen as a wonderful advance in human understanding of the world in which we live or as something misleading and dangerous, no rational person can go back to a pre-Darwinian way of thinking. The same applies to the ideas of Karl Marx and Sigmund Freud. Both were atheists, with ideas which contradicted established Christian thought, and both were immensely influential. Even if some aspects of their thinking were mistaken, it impossible to go back to a pre-Marxist or a pre-Freudian way of thinking. Christianity needs to learn to co-exist with other ideas, whether in the realm of astronomy or geology or economics or politics or psychology or anything else. Ideally Christians will learn something of value from them.

Chapter 11

Theology in the Twentieth Century

The Roman Catholic church reacted to the threat of the Enlightenment by asserting the authority of the pope, and the first striking example of this was in 1854, when Pius IX, whose pontificate lasted nearly thirty-two years, from 1846 until 1878, proclaimed the doctrine of the immaculate conception of the Blessed Virgin Mary. Mary was revered by many pious Catholics as "full of grace" – *gratia plena*, a translation by Jerome at the end of the fourth century of the Greek word *kecharitomene*, which Erasmus, much later, thought better translated as "highly favoured". Literally it means "You who have been graced", and how one translates it makes a big difference.

The idea that Mary was "full of grace" had led to her being seen by some Catholics as the "mediatrix of all graces", and even as the co-redemtrix of the world with Jesus. But there had always been some disagreement among theologians about the appropriate theological position of Mary. The Council of Ephesus back in 431 had been dominated by the question of whether she should be described as *Theotokos*, God-bearer, or merely as *Christotokos*, Christbearer.

Thomas Aquinas in the middle of the thirteenth century believed that she was affected by original sin as much as any other person, but another important medieval theologian, Duns Scotus (1266–1308), argued that she was *immaculata*, "free from sin" from the moment of her conception. There was no scriptural authority for such a belief, but in 1854 it was asserted as a matter of papal authority.

Then ten years later Pius IX set out his opposition to all things modern in a *Syllabus of Errors*, condemning liberalism, socialism, communism, the separation of church and state, the freedom of the press, freedom of religion, civil marriage and secular education. After another six years, in 1870, at a council known as the First Vatican Council, the doctrine of papal infallibility was proclaimed. That is, it was made an essential article of faith that if the pope spoke *ex cathedra*, from the throne of St Peter, on a matter of faith or morals, his views were infallibly true, as much as if they had been uttered by God Himself.

During the early twentieth century, during the pontificate of Pius X, from 1903 until 1914, there was an extension of opposition to all things modern, and Roman Catholic bishops, priests and teachers were required to take an anti-modernist oath. Speculation was discouraged, and in 1950 Pope Pius XII made another infallible pronouncement, proclaiming the doctrine of the bodily assumption of the Blessed Virgin Mary. Believing that Mary had been physically "assumed", or raised up, into heaven was now, like the doctrine of her immaculate conception and the doctrine of papal infallibility, "altogether necessary for salvation".

Some Protestants were equally authoritarian, though in their case it was the Bible that was seen as the source of infallible authority. In 1895 a group of Protestants from a wide range of denominations, but who all thought of themselves as evangelicals, met at a Bible conference at Niagara, on the border of the USA and Canada, and drew up a statement of what they saw as the five fundamentals of the Christian religion: "[T]he Bible is the Word of God and cannot err; Jesus is God; he was born of a virgin; he suffered and was punished on the cross as a substitute for sinful mankind; Christians should expect his imminent return in glory to bring about the bodily resurrection of those of the dead who have been saved". These five points were the "fundamentals", and anyone who did not assent to them was not a true Christian.

When one looks at the way Jesus had criticized the religious leaders of his own time, one can scarcely avoid feeling that he would have been similarly critical of many of the religious leaders of the late nineteenth and early twentieth centuries, both Roman Catholic and evangelical. In the event neither contributed anything of value to the development of Christian ideas. Both fell back on assertions of authority. They had millions of followers, of course, and many of those followers no doubt trusted in the teaching and example of Jesus and lived good lives seeking to put their faith into practice. But the leadership of both the Roman Catholic church and the evangelical alliance left much to be desired.

Thus the development of theology in the twentieth century came to be the preserve of traditional Protestants, and probably the most distinguished of those theologians was the Swiss Karl Barth (1886–1968) who over more than thirty years produced a massive account of *Church Dogmatics*, though he did not live to finish it. It is widely seen by other theologians as a systematic account of the best of Protestant theology, with a viewpoint often referred to as neo-orthodoxy. It is the nearest thing there is to a Protestant equivalent of the *Summa Theologica* of Thomas Aquinas. The one thing which is significantly new in it is the distinction Barth draws between the self-revelation of God in the life and crucifixion of Jesus and the human constructions of religion, such as the churches, which, he believed, too often got in the way of following Christ.

In the middle of the twentieth century a number of theologians who had in common that they were either German or of German extraction, sought new ways of understanding and expressing the Christian faith. One particularly important German theologian of the mid-twentieth century was Rudolf Bultmann. Three other Germans, Martin Niemöller, Dietrich Bonhoeffer and Jürgen Moltmann, all had something worthwhile to say and wrote about Christianity as a result of their experiences in the Nazi era of 1933 until 1945. Two more theologians, Reinhold Niebuhr and Paul Tillich, were Americans of German origin.

Niebuhr, the son of a German immigrant into the USA, was born there and taught at the Union Theological Seminary in New York for more than thirty years. Tillich, who fled from the Nazis to the USA in 1933, joined Niebuhr at the Union Theological Seminary.

All six of them had insights which are worth considering. Rudolf Bultmann was a Lutheran who was born in 1884 and became the professor of New Testament at Marburg University in 1921. He avoided any involvement in politics throughout the Nazi years and continued with his work at Marburg until he retired in 1951. As early as 1941 he suggested in an essay called *New Testament and Mythology* that it was time to demythologize the Christian story. His contention was that the New Testament writers, seeking to convey their sense of awe and wonder at the life and work of Jesus of Nazareth, had used mythological language to convey that sense. Thus they wrote of angels and demons, of pre-existence and incarnation, of divine intervention, of ascent and descent between heaven and Earth. Too often, suggested Bultmann, Christians lose sight of the scandal of the crucifixion, because it is hidden behind a lot of mythology which is now irrelevant.

The mythology, Bultmann suggested, had made good sense to many previous generations of Christians. But understanding of the universe had changed dramatically since the time of Newton, and the mythology was no longer credible. Thus the resurrection, he argued, took place in the subjective experience of the disciples, not in history as we now understand it. Jesus was indeed raised, but in a mythological or metaphorical sense. Whether particular events are literally true or not, said Bultmann, echoing the third-century teaching of Origen, does not matter. What matters is the proclamation of the gospel, the good news.

Paul Tillich, who was born two years later in 1886, was another German Protestant theologian, and had been professor of theology at Frankfurt University before finding refuge in the USA in 1933. He tried to rethink the idea of God in the twentieth century, and has been seen as the most significant American theologian since Jonathan Edwards in the eighteenth century. He had much in common with Bultmann and appreciated that human experience necessarily varies from one culture to another, both in time and place. He also realised that this must affect theological understanding.

In particular he tackled the issue that the modern understanding of the universe had produced for many people a problem with the idea of the existence of God. It no longer made sense to locate God somewhere up in the heavens, or "out there", and there are difficulties in thinking of God as a "person", since, if the word "person" means something recognizable, then God would need to be located in a particular place. In a sermon first published in England in 1949 he argued that what clearly does exist is something which can be described as "the infinite and inexhaustible depth and ground of all being", and that, suggested Tillich, is God. The question of whether or not God exists is, he argued, the wrong question. The appropriate question is how we should respond to "the infinite and inexhaustible depth and ground of all being".

Tillich was clearly thinking along the same lines as Bultmann when he tackled the problem of how to explain what Paul in the first century had described in the sixth chapter of his letter to the Ephesians as wrestling "not against flesh and blood, but against principalities, against powers, against the rulers of the darkness of this world". Tillich saw that the battle was not against those external, or objective, forces of evil, such as demons, with which early Christians had felt they had to contend, but rather was one against the internal, or subjective, forces, such as depression and paranoia, which corrupt and distort human lives. Salvation could be a matter of being freed from enslavement to such forces and being free to live life abundantly. Mary Magdalen was a good example of someone who was seen as suffering from "evil spirits and infirmities", but whose life was transformed by Jesus, who, in the language of the time, caused seven devils to leave her.

Similarly important was Reinhold Niebuhr, who was born in 1892 in the USA. He tackled the problem that moral issues are usually far from simple and argued that the choice for Christians is often not so much between right and wrong as between what is ideal and what is practical. On the one hand Christians see peace and mercy, and even poverty, as noble ideals. On the other hand, most believed that it was right to fight Nazi Germany, imprison criminals, and work hard to accumulate wealth. So did Niebuhr. But he was aware of the contradictions and sought to resolve them.

For example, Niebuhr was clear that, while society needs mercy, mercy only makes sense in the context of justice. Christians would often be faced with difficult decisions and would need to exercise their judgement in the light of the teaching of Jesus. But they could easily be wrong. It was therefore all the more important to cultivate humility and avoid any sense of moral superiority. They should take such action as appeared to be appropriate, but they should recognise their own fallibility and forgive the sins of others as they themselves would wish to be forgiven.

Niebuhr is most remembered for what is called *The Serenity Prayer*, which begins, "God grant me the serenity to accept the things I cannot change, courage to change the things I can, and wisdom to know the difference". Praying in that way should ideally help a person to find the necessary serenity, courage and wisdom to cope with life. But there are no guarantees.

Martin Niemöller, who was born in the same year as Niebuhr, is memorable for both his personal views and his example rather than for any theological insights. He was a successful U-boat commander during the First World War, trained as a Lutheran pastor afterwards, and although a fervent nationalist became one of the leaders of the Confessing Church which opposed Nazism. He spent seven years imprisoned in concentration camps, but was freed by American forces shortly before the end of the war.

He had at first welcomed the rise of the Nazi Party, and later confessed that Hitler's anti-Semitism was only a more extreme form of his own prejudice at the time. Shortly after the war, he made a statement in which he declined to claim innocence in respect of the rise of the Nazis: "First they came for the Communists, but I was not a Communist, so I said nothing. Then they came for the Social Democrats, but I was not a Social Democrat, so I did nothing. Then they came for the trade unionists, but I was not a trade unionist. And then they came for the Jews, but I was not a Jew, so I did little. Then, when they came for me, there was no one left to stand up for me".

He survived to become a Lutheran bishop and in relatively old age became a committed pacifist. He remembered how his father had told him as a child that the best rule for life was to behave as if the man next to you was Jesus Christ. He also remembered ordering torpedo tubes to be fired at British merchant ships in the First World War, and now he felt that, if he had imagined the man next to him to be Jesus Christ, he could not have done that.

Dietrich Bonhoeffer was fourteen years younger than Niemöller. He was born in 1906 and as a young man went abroad to study under Reinhold Niebuhr in New York. While there he began to see the importance of seeing things "from below" – from the perspective of those who suffer oppression. He returned to Germany and was a Lutheran minister in his twenties when the Nazis came to power. He joined Niemöller in forming the Confessing Church, was arrested in April 1943 and spent the next year and a half in prison.

While imprisoned Bonhoèffer reflected on and wrote about the role of the church in society and came to believe that, contrary to the traditional idea of God as almighty, the Bible pointed us towards the idea of the powerlessness of God in the world, something symbolised by the suffering of Jesus on the cross. It was, he believed, precisely because God is weak and powerless that He can suffer alongside us and, in so doing, help us. Thus the strength of the Christian God lies not in power but in love and compassion, sharing in the pain and distress of mankind throughout history.

One of his most important insights was that, while the Church had down the ages assumed that human beings feel within them a need for religion, now it seemed possible that many people felt that they could live their lives without religion. Many had neither any sense of sin nor any feeling that they either wanted or needed salvation. He was clearly influenced by the thoughts of Karl Barth as he began to wonder about the possibility of "religionless Christianity" in a future "world come of age". Back in the first century Paul had called mankind to follow Jesus without any need to be circumcised. In the twentieth century Bonhoeffer was wondering if it would be possible to follow Jesus without any need for religion.

Just how far he would have developed these ideas we cannot be sure, for he did not live long enough to work them out fully. But it seems probable that he was not envisaging a world without Christian congregations, but rather one in which "religion" was less significant than the teaching of Jesus. It should be possible, he seems to have thought, to be a Christian without being committed to doctrines such as those of atonement and the ascension, or even the incarnation and the resurrection. A year and a half after being imprisoned he was transferred to a concentration camp, where he was executed in April 1945, just as Nazism was being defeated.

Jürgen Moltmann was born twenty years later, in 1926. As a teenager he was fascinated by Einstein's ideas about relativity and intended studying mathematics at university. But he was drafted into the German army in 1943, when he was still sixteen, and during the years from 1945 until 1947, as a prisoner of war of the British, he turned to Christianity. He returned to Germany to study theology and in 1967 became the professor of systematic theology at Tübingen University, where he remained until he retired in 1994. It is his thinking about both suffering and hope which is important.

He picked up Bonhoeffer's idea that God could help mankind not by the exercise of power but by sharing in the pain and distress which so many human beings suffered. The idea that God could suffer had been condemned in the fourth century as the heresy of *patripassianism*. But Moltmann's own experiences led him to believe that a God who was indifferent to the large-scale suffering of the warfare of 1914–1945 was scarcely credible. He was influenced not only by Bonhoeffer but also by Martin Luther's "theology of the cross". Luther, while believing that God should be seen as a glorious and almighty being, had spoken of God the Father sharing in the suffering of the crucified Christ, and he saw the cross as the source of knowledge about who God is and how He saves.

In *The Crucified God* in 1974 Moltmann argued that a God who could not suffer would be an insensitive being who could not love either, and that when Jesus suffered the physical and emotional agony of dying on the cross, the Father suffered with him. The word "compassion" means "to suffer with" the sufferer. The compassionate God was there when the suffering of Jesus was made worse by the belief that God had forsaken him, and that same God shares in all human suffering. The fact that *patripassianism* had been condemned by the early Church as a heresy was not an adequate reason, Moltmann thought, for believing in the twentieth century in the inability of God to suffer. To love involves suffering with the sufferings of the beloved. Thus, if anyone who is faced with suffering in the modern world asks where God is, the answer is that "He is there, suffering with the sufferer".

Moltmann also argued for the need to rediscover the importance of Hope in Christian lives. Hope, he appreciated, is the most neglected of Paul's three great theological virtues: Faith, Hope and Charity, or Love. So he wanted Christians to share in hope for humanity through the grace of a loving God who shares in their suffering. A thousand years earlier Anselm had said, "I believe in order that I may understand". Moltmann said, "I hope in order that I may understand".

It may well take time for these ideas to trickle down to the clergy of the various Christian denominations, and even longer for them to trickle down to Christian congregations. But they are part of our heritage, together with the Bible and other books beyond number, together with cathedrals and parish churches and meeting houses, together with requiem masses, settings of the passion, and hymns, together with religious paintings and sculpture.

Meanwhile, a particularly important development in twentieth-century Christian theology was being worked out in the southern continent of America in ways which reflected the problems of that area. The work culminated in 1968 in a congress of the Roman Catholic bishops of Latin America in Colombia, at which they acknowledged that their church had too often sided with oppressive regimes, and they went on to declare that in future it would be on the side of the poor.

A number of what were described as liberation theologians wrote persuasively about how God was on the side of the poor, and they argued that Christian mission needed to begin with the "view from below", recognising the suffering and distress of the poor and the oppressed, and seeing things from their viewpoint. The job of the church, they argued, was not to explain the world but to transform it.

They were critical of traditional theology, which they saw as too often being concerned with issues having no relationship to social problems. For centuries theology at its best had followed the view succinctly put by Bernard of Clairvaux in the twelfth century that "contemplation must issue in action". But too often contemplation had been followed by more contemplation, as theologians agonized over and dissected details of the faith while neglecting action to care for the poor and oppressed. Now, asserted the liberation theologians, it should be the other way round. What was needed was action to transform the world. Only afterwards would it make sense to reflect critically on what had been done and consider how, in the light of the gospel, one might act better to transform the world. Reflection without prior action, they argued, was barren.

The liberation theologians were clearly and unequivocally opposed to the view that one should keep religion out of politics. Politics is to do with the relationships between human beings in society, and that, they believed, should be at the heart of religion, and therefore of theology as well. If it was the job of the church to transform the world for the better, Christians should be prepared to take action on behalf of the poor and oppressed.

They frequently made use of the analysis by Karl Marx of the problems of modern society, and they made use of Marxist ideas about how an unjust political system could be overthrown and replaced by something better. Inevitably they were criticized for their use of Marxism, since Karl Marx was a non-Christian, but their reply was that they were doing no more than Thomas Aquinas had done when he made use of the ideas of the pre-Christian Aristotle in developing his theology.

Moreover, the distortion of Marxism by the Bolsheviks in Russia should not lead, they believed, to a failure to make use of those ideas in Marxism which were relevant to the situation in Latin America. The liberation theologians were clearly on strong ground when they appealed to the gospels for evidence that Jesus was on the side of the poor and against those who abused their power and wealth in oppressing the poor. They could also quote the prophet Amos, who condemned the rich, describing them as "cows of Bashan... who oppress the poor and crush the destitute", and who hoped for a time when the rich would be "pitched on a dunghill".

The liberation theologians were also criticized on the grounds that they were more concerned with social, political and economic problems than with the world of the spirit, and were confusing liberation with salvation, or getting into a right relationship with God. After all, those who are liberated will not necessarily use their freedom well. But they could and did reply that Jesus was concerned with the abuse of power and wealth, and the possibility that those who were liberated would misuse their freedom did not absolve the church from facing the question of what Christians should do about social, political and economic problems, and how they should seek to see God's will done "on Earth as it is in heaven".

Another separate development, in this case in the USA, was black theology. That also came to the fore in the 1960s and 1970s, and although it seemed to develop quite separately from the liberation theology of Latin America and was largely a Protestant rather than a Roman Catholic movement, it was also concerned with the issue of liberation. Large numbers of black men and women had been enslaved in north America ever since colonial times, and although in 1863, during the American Civil War, they had been "emancipated", or freed from slavery, black men and women in the USA, as well as very large numbers of people of mixed race, still faced discrimination on a scale which understandably caused bitter resentment.

Many, probably most, were Christians, but their churches both in the North and the South were separate from those of their white fellow-citizens. Their church leaders could point to the liberation of the Hebrew slaves described in the book of Exodus, when Moses had told Pharaoh to "let my people go". Like the liberation theologians they could appeal to the prophets, and they could point to the prophetic words of Mary, the mother of Jesus: "He hath put down the mighty from their seat and hath exalted the humble and meek. He hath filled the hungry with good things, and the rich he hath sent empty away". The traditional but questionable translation of those words into the past tense tends, but only tends, to obscure their force.

Meanwhile, a third movement concerning liberation was developing. In this case it was women's liberation, which was aimed at changing the position of women in society as a whole. It was not primarily a Christian movement, but one element in it was, and that was concerned with the position of women in the church. Women clearly played an important part in the early church, but Paul wrote to the Christians at Corinth saying that women should not be allowed to speak in church, and he wrote to Timothy saying that he did not allow them to teach and did not put them in positions of authority over men. Then, as the church became an established part of the Roman Empire and accepted the established secular culture in which women were clearly subordinate to men, Paul's comments were used down the centuries to justify that.

But Paul was writing about particular circumstances and about the problems in his own time. He was influenced by the culture he had inherited as well as by the teaching of Jesus, and he accepted the institution of slavery as well as the subordination of women. His teaching, like that of Jesus, was above all about an attitude of mind and it pointed towards the future. It would take nearly two thousand years before the church came out unequivocally against slavery, and the question of the appropriate position of women in relation to men still for many people remains unresolved.

By the second half of the twentieth century there was a widespread demand for women to be ordained as priests and consecrated as bishops. It was an issue which raised theological issues about the nature of the church and, at a time when there was much talk of ecumenism and the search for Christian unity, decisions about whether or not it was right to go ahead with the ordination of women depended not just on the merits of the issue itself but also on, for example, whether or not it was right to go ahead when doing so would cause a breach with another church. The main arguments against women holding positions of leadership in the church were always those to be found in the writings of Paul, but another was that Jesus and his apostles were all men, and that, it was contended, was a clear indication of how Jesus expected his church to be. But the apostles were also all Jewish, and there had never been a requirement that all church leaders should be Jewish. Why, it was asked, should there be a requirement that they should all be men?

Disagreement continued, as it so often had in the past, about a vast range of theological, liturgical, pastoral and practical issues. But as the church reached the third millennium after Christ, there could be no doubt that someone who was a black woman and poor would usually have a far worse quality of life than someone who was a white man and rich. Paul had written to the Christians of Galatia in about AD 56 that there is "neither Jew nor Greek, neither bond nor free, neither male nor female, for you are all one in Christ Jesus". Two thousand years later a poster in the USA proclaimed that "God is black", and on it someone added "and she's a woman". Clearly there were issues waiting to be resolved.

The range of issues brought to the fore by the feminist movement raised the theological issue of how far it is helpful nowadays to speak of God as "father", as Jesus had done, rather than as "mother". It does not need much thought to realise that to attribute sexuality to the being people think of as God does not make sense. The point of speaking of God as "father" was that it conveyed the idea of a being with a paternal loving-care for his creation. But might one not just as well speak of God as "mother", who could similarly be seen as a being with maternal loving-care for her creation? Probably the best reason one can give for the use of the word "father" is that Jesus used it and we have got used to it.

Christianity in its traditional Roman Catholic and Orthodox forms, as well as in its various Protestant, evangelical, fundamentalist and charismatic forms, remains influential in much of the world. Some Christians welcome new ideas, but others fear them. Ideas have power. The ideas of Jesus of Nazareth transformed the world. The ideas of some of his followers (Paul of Tarsus, Augustine of Hippo, Benedict of Nursia, Francis of Assisi, Luther, Calvin, Wesley, for example) have also been transformative. Perhaps in the long run the combined ideas of Barth, Bultmann, Tillich, Niebuhr, Niemöller, Bonhoeffer and Moltmann, as well as those theologians of the second half of the twentieth century who were concerned with such issues as the liberation of the poor and equal rights for people of any race or gender, will similarly transform understanding and lead Christians closer to appreciating what most matters in the teaching and example of Jesus of Nazareth, and how they should seek to put his teaching and example into action.

Chapter 12

Into the Third Millennium

As the Christian church moved into the third millennium it was the largest of the world's religions, with roughly a third of the population of the world attached to one or another of the Christian churches. The largest of those churches was the Roman Catholic church, which reached throughout the world. Then there were the various national churches, including the Russian Orthodox, which had emerged after years of persecution in the Bolshevik USSR, the Church of England and the Lutheran churches of Scandinavia. In the eastern Mediterranean Orthodox churches still survived under either Muslim or secular governments. There were also those Protestant churches which had their origins in the Reformation in Western Europe in the sixteenth century and had spread across the Atlantic to the USA. Meanwhile, especially in the African continent, there were innumerable other Christian sects, each of which could interpret the gospel in its own way.

Christians were not only divided into numerous different denominations, churches or sects. They also differed widely in their beliefs – so much so that it is scarcely possible to find a satisfactory answer to the question, "What do Christians believe?" or "How do Christians think about things?" One can explain what particular groups believe, but it is difficult to discern something that is believed by all.

Perhaps the most obvious doctrine which is believed by most Christians early in the third millennium is the doctrine of the trinity. That is, while they worship a being who is usually referred to as God and often as God the Father, they are also devoted to the memory of Jesus of Nazareth, and he is seen as associated with God the Father in a trinity, whose third person is the Holy Spirit. Insofar as this gives the message that the God whom Christians worship is a loving interrelationship between God the Father, Jesus Christ and the Holy Spirit, it is an idea, or doctrine, of value to many Christians. But it can be misused if it is accepted in the manner of a prejudice, with little understanding of its significance. Even worse is the situation in which a group's failure to adhere to it is used as the reason for excluding them from inter-communion with other Christians.

Archbishop William Temple of Canterbury encountered that problem in 1942 when inaugurating the British Council of Churches. Although the council was the fruit of the ecumenical movement, which was aimed at bringing the various Christian denominations closer together, there was some opposition to admitting the Unitarians, on the grounds that they did not accept the doctrine of the trinity. William Temple made the case for including them. First, the aim of the council was to be inclusive rather than exclusive. Secondly, there were considerable tracts of England where there were large numbers of Unitarians, and people in those areas would simply not understand their exclusion. Thirdly, no one had argued for the exclusion of the Quakers, and it would be strange to include a group which had no doctrine of the Godhead, while excluding one which had a mistaken doctrine. At the time his argument carried the day, but eighty years later Unitarians, and Quakers as well, are often excluded from ecumenical groups by those who require giving assent to the doctrine of the trinity as a requirement for being accepted as a Christian.

Just as there is widespread acceptance among Christians of the doctrine of the trinity, similarly there is widespread acceptance of the doctrines of the incarnation, the belief that Jesus was divine wisdom in human form, the resurrection, the belief that he rose from the dead after his crucifixion, and the ascension, the belief that he ascended into heaven forty days later. But some people who still consider themselves to be

Christians question the truth of the doctrine of the incarnation, even more see the stories relating to the resurrection as metaphorically rather than literally true, and many see the story of the ascension as implausible.

A relatively minor theological issue has helped to cause division in the world-wide Christian church ever since 1014, when Pope Benedict VIII approved the inclusion in the Nicene creed of the word *filioque*, which literally means "and the son". The Nicene creed as agreed at the Council of Constantinople in 381 had declared that the Holy Spirit proceeded "from the Father", the Father being seen as the ultimate source of all creation, but in the Catholic west it came to be asserted that the procession of the Holy Spirit was "from the Father and the Son". In itself it is a small point. The real problem was that the Bishop of Rome, the pope, was claiming the right to alter a creed which had been agreed in an ecumenical council. The view in the east was that although the pope was *primus inter pares*, "first among equals", among the patriarchs of Christendom, he did not have the authority to over-rule all the others.

That problem continues. The issue of authority has divided the Orthodox east from the Catholic west ever since. Over the centuries the west got used to the inclusion of the *filioque* clause, so that at the time of the Reformation it was not an issue, and both Luther and Calvin accepted the Nicene creed in its western form. Today the issue of the *filioque* clause is entirely unimportant to most Christians and matters only to a few church leaders. In the late twentieth century some Protestant churches considered dropping it, and the episcopal church of Scotland actually did so.

There were two other problems with the Nicene creed by the twenty-first century. One was that Jesus was said to be "of one substance with the Father". That had been an issue of immense importance in the fourth century, but now that few people think in Aristotelian terms about "substance", it has long ceased to have any significance. Church leaders have tried to avoid the problem by, for example, changing the wording to "of one being with the Father", but the question of whether Jesus was "of one substance with the Father" or "of a similar substance", which tore the Church apart in the fourth century, is now of no more significance to most Christians than the *filioque* clause.

The other problem with the Nicene creed is far more important. Every Sunday millions of Christians throughout the world declare that they believe in "everlasting life", but few have a clear idea of what is meant by that. No rational person can in the third millennium believe that it means an eternity in which the community of saints do nothing but praise God in a place in the sky known as heaven, while those not among the elect spend eternity under the ground in hell, being persecuted by demons. What it does mean is beyond human comprehension, and although speaking of "eternal life" is preferable to speaking of "everlasting life", that does not solve the problem. Jesus had told his followers that there were many resting places in his Father's house, and Paul declared that "this corruptible must put on incorruption". While each of those statements can be reassuring, neither of them goes far towards answering the question of what happens when people die.

No one can know with any certainty what happens to the human body, soul or spirit when a human being dies, and possibly the most helpful thought about this came from the German philosopher Schopenhauer, who recognised that by the nineteenth century many people believed that there would be nothing after death – nothing at all. But, he pointed out, "nothing" only has meaning within the context of known human experience, and "nothing" after death would bear no resemblance to the nothing that any of us has either experienced or thought about.

There remains the problem with each of these disputes over the Nicene creed that they are many centuries out of date and the question of whether or not to include something in the creed is far more an issue of authority in the church than one of theology. As theological issues they now have little or, in the case of the first two, no significance. The main case for continuing to include them is that the church is committed to upholding "the ancient formularies of the church", which is another way of saying that, however much theological thinking has moved on, and however mistaken is what was agreed at Nicaea in 325 and Constantinople in 381, Christians are expected to give it regular public assent.

Another issue over which there is disagreement is what are known as the sacraments. These had been important to Christians ever since the days of the early church and are often described as "outward and visible signs of inward invisible grace". By the time of the religious controversies of the seventeenth century the Roman Catholic church taught that there were seven sacraments: baptism, confirmation, the eucharist (or mass), penance, marriage, ordination and extreme unction, the last of which was the practice of anointing someone who was dying with consecrated oil.

But Luther argued that only baptism and the eucharist, both of which had been instituted by the Lord (*dominus*), could be regarded as true, or dominical, sacraments, and that view came to be generally accepted in Protestant churches. Confirmation, penance, marriage, ordination and extreme unction might, or might not, have their own importance, but Protestants did not regard them as sacraments. They did generally accept both baptism and the eucharist.

There was disagreement, not only between Catholics and Protestants but also among Protestants about the sacrament of baptism. It was traditionally seen as a public sign that a child now belonged to the Christian community. Paul had argued near the beginning of the second chapter of his letter to the Colossians that it was the Christian equivalent of what circumcision had been for the Jews, and the practice had the double merit that, unlike circumcision, it involved no shedding of blood and also applied to female as well as male children.

There is no explicit biblical justification for infant baptism, nor is there any clear evidence that it was the practice in the early church, so while some Christians see it as a sacrament remitting original sin (with the necessary consequence, if it does, that an unbaptised tiny baby is doomed to eternal damnation), many others have always seen it as a public gesture of the acceptance of the child into the Christian community.

The distinctive thing about the Baptist church is that Baptists believe that people should only be baptised after they are adult and have "come to faith", and in the twentieth century the Swiss Calvinist theologian Karl Barth criticized the practice of infant baptism partly because it lacks biblical justification, but more importantly because it tends to reduce baptism to a social custom rather than marking the beginning of an individual's response to the grace of God. Nevertheless, the vast majority of Christians continue to accept infant baptism as normal practice in a Christian, or partly Christian, community.

There was even more disagreement among Christians about the other dominical sacrament: the eucharist. Quite early in the history of the church Christians were meeting to give thanks for the life and sacrifice on the cross of their Lord and Saviour, Jesus Christ. They would eat bread and drink wine in remembrance of him, though just what they believed about it for the first millennium and a half of the Christian church is difficult to know. But in the middle of the sixteenth century the Roman Catholic church declared that Christians were required to believe that the bread and wine, on being consecrated, became *veriter, realiter, substantialiter,* "truly, really and substantially", the actual flesh and blood of Jesus.

Luther could not accept this doctrine of transubstantiation, but nevertheless believed in the real presence of God in the sacraments. Meanwhile the Swiss reformer Huldreich Zwingli described the bread and wine as *nuda signa*, "bare signs", of Jesus, though he also saw them as powerful reminders of Christ's death on the cross. Calvin's view was that they should be seen as "sure, certain and effective signs" of Christ's crucified body. Conflict over the issue was bitter, but none of them, not even the Roman Catholics, claimed that the physical characteristics of the bread and wine changed. The differences are really linguistic ones, and the best statement of eucharistic theology to emerge from the bitter conflicts of the sixteenth century is a couplet attributed to Queen Elizabeth I of England:

His was the Word that spake it. He took the bread and brake it,
And what his words do make it, that I believe and take it.

Roman Catholics and Protestants also disagree about the status of the Bible. Catholics stress that it was the church which gave authority to those scriptures which it decided to include in the Bible. Protestants are more inclined to argue that the church was giving its assent to the authority which the scriptures already possessed. Both views are possible. In the end, whether one emphasizes the authority of the scriptures or of the church depends on one's own conscience and understanding, or simply on how one was brought up.

There were similar divisions among Christians over moral issues. They probably agree that you should "love the Lord you God with all your heart and with all your soul and with all your strength and with all your mind, and your neighbour as yourself". But there is little agreement on how to translate that into practice. Christians include pacifists as well as those who see going to war as justifiable under particular circumstances. There are those whose belief in the sanctity of life causes them to oppose all abortion or assisted dying. But there are others who believe that all women should have the right to choose when to have an abortion, and that the elderly and infirm should both be allowed to choose when to die and assisted in doing so. Such disagreements apply to a range of other moral issues.

There is widespread agreement among Christians about the desirability of prayer, and Christians seem to be agreed about the importance of worshipping God, giving thanks for all the benefits one receives in life, and examining one's own conscience – in some form confessing, or acknowledging, one's faults and seeking to put right any wrong one has done. Far more difficult is the issue of intercessory prayer. Some Christians believe that God listens to individual prayers and always answers them, though not necessarily as the person praying intended or wanted. But they appear to believe that, if only people pray hard enough and with sufficient faith, then God can be persuaded to end a drought or a famine or a war, or be persuaded to deflect bullets and check the growth of cancer cells.

There is also, however, a long tradition of a very different approach to prayer which reaches all the way back to Jesus praying about getting our relationships right with God and with each other. It is a tradition which includes Origen in the third century telling us not to pray for the cool of spring in the heat of summer, Augustine of Hippo warning his congregations that they should not to try to change God's unalterable will but rather should seek to align their wills to his, Bernard of Clairvaux in the twelfth century teaching that contemplation must issue in action, Archbishop Cranmer's collects in the sixteenth century, the Danish theologian and philosopher Søren Kierkegaard arguing in the nineteenth century that the function of prayer is not to influence God but rather to change the nature of the one who prays, and then in the twentieth century the scientist and theologian John Polkinghorne arguing, as Augustine had, that we should be seeking to align ourselves with the will of God rather than presuming to tell Him what to do.

Meanwhile Old Testament scholars have shown how the Bible is a collection of varied writings, such as ancient myths, early history, tribal law, love poetry and religious thinking, and they have disturbed traditional thinking. There were always some who believed that the Bible was the inspired work of God, dictated by him and arranged with divine perfection. But, for example, the Book of Ruth is placed far too early. It makes the point that not all foreign wives were bad, in reply to the books of Ezra and Nehemiah, which are placed far later in the Bible and describe how those returning from exile in Babylon told the Jews to "put away your foreign wives". It is a beautiful story, and its heroine, Ruth, the great-grandmother of King David, is a Moabitess. But it was misplaced between Judges and the First Book of Samuel because it begins with the words, "Now it came to pass in the days when the judges ruled..."

The rules in the Old Testament about burnt offerings, selling one's daughter into slavery and stoning to death have long been superseded by the teaching of Jesus, and the stories in the Old Testament should not be seen as models of how we should behave. When Abraham in chapter two of Genesis prepares to sacrifice his son, and when Jephthah in chapter eleven of Judges does sacrifice his daughter, we should not feel, "How wonderful that they loved God so much that they were prepared to burn their children to death!" Nor should we feel that they were nothing but evil child abusers. We should recognise that the past is a different country, where they did things differently, and we should seek to understand – not uphold the right and condemn the wrong, but just try to understand a bit better.

Old Testament scholars showed how one's understanding can be affected by translation. In the King James version of the Bible the fourteenth verse of the seventh chapter of Isaiah is translated, "Behold, a virgin shall conceive and bear a son...", but when the revised standard version of the Old Testament was published in 1952, it read, "Behold a young woman shall conceive…" The reason for the change was not that the revisers were denying the virgin birth of Jesus, but rather that they were striving for accuracy. The Hebrew word *almah* can be translated variously as "young woman", "maiden", "virgin" or "teenage girl". But there is another Hebrew word, *betulah*, which quite specifically means "virgin". If Isaiah had wanted to say "virgin", he could have used that. But he did not. So the revisers opted for the neutral translation, "young woman". That offended both Protestant evangelicals and Roman Catholics, and in 2001 the evangelicals produced an alternative Bible which restored the word "virgin", and in 2006 the Roman Catholics did the same.

New Testament scholars also faced problems of translation. The language Jesus and his disciples spoke was Aramaic, but the gospels and all the letters and other books which make up the New Testament are written in Greek. They were later translated into other languages, sometimes many centuries later. The "Authorized", or King James, version in English, for example, was produced in 1611, more than one and a half millennia after the originals were written. Since the New Testament was written in Greek, names in it, of course, appear in Greek. Jesus was the Greek version (*Iesos*) of the ancient Hebrew name Joshua, which meant "the Lord Saves". Christ was the Greek version (*Kristos*) of the Hebrew word Messiah, which means "the Anointed One". Knowing that can make a difference to one's understanding of the text.

There is a story in the third chapter of the Acts of the Apostles of how Peter was arrested and brought before the high priest, who asks him, "By what name, or by what power" he had cured a lame man. Peter replied that it was "by the name of Jesus Christ of Nazareth, whom you crucified, and whom God raised from the dead". He added a comment which is usually translated, "There is no other name under heaven given among men by which we must be saved" (Acts chapter 4 verse 12). But the Greek word *dei*, which is here translated as "must", also means "it is appropriate", and that makes particularly good sense here, for Jesus's name meant "the Lord saves", and Peter was saying that it was appropriate that we should be saved by the name of Jesus, or Joshua, because that was precisely what the name meant. It can be seen as first-century Jewish humour. But that is not an explanation which commends itself to those who want to view it as an exclusive statement that those who do not toe the official Christian line will be damned.

Most of the Christian churches in the twentieth century did not react well to biblical criticism or to other aspects of modern scholarship, any more than they had reacted well to the scientific revolution or the thinking of the Enlightenment. Some individuals welcomed the new insights provided by modern theologians, but most of those ideas were generally seen as threats to established beliefs and were not passed down as far as the congregations, of whatever denomination.

Meanwhile, many people who did not count themselves as Christians valued much of their inherited Christian tradition. The accumulated stories in both the Old and the New Testaments, not least the stories surrounding the birth of Jesus and those about the events leading up to his crucifixion and suffering on the cross, are part of our cultural heritage. So are the many medieval cathedrals and parish churches, the paintings and sculptures, requiem masses, settings of the passion, hymns and Christmas carols, and the liturgy used in church services. They all tell something of mankind's struggle to rise above the material world and seek to make contact with whatever may be beyond.

Even the traditional teaching of the church on matters of doctrine is part of our cultural heritage. But as education and freedom of choice advanced, so did a rising tide of scepticism about the old certainties. That could already be discerned in the eighteenth century, it swelled in the nineteenth, and by the middle of the twentieth century the attitude of untold thousands of Europeans can be seen encapsulated in the words of the two men who presided over the government of Great Britain from 1940 until 1955. Winston Churchill said of himself, "I am not a pillar of the church. I am more of a flying buttress: I support it from the outside". Clement Attlee, when asked towards the end of his life about his attitude to Christianity, replied with characteristic succinctness, "I believe in the ethics, but not the mumbo-jumbo".

Both tried to live their own lives and also to lead Great Britain in accordance with the moral code handed down from Jesus, even if they interpreted it differently; and they respected, liked and admired each other. But neither presumed to call himself a Christian, because they did not believe, and therefore would not give public assent to, the various doctrines which the church required its members to accept. Much the same was true of hundreds of thousands of others, and meanwhile the various denominations of the church did not themselves agree about those doctrines.

The church had done much to contribute to bringing that situation about. Instead of rejoicing at the spread of education and welcoming the riches of theological thinking in the twentieth century, leaders of the church usually clung to the certainties of the past. Faced with a decline in membership they sought to increase the numbers attending church on Sundays by proclaiming those old certainties. Faced with threats to its reputation, as when priests were guilty of child abuse, they too often tried to protect its reputation rather than care for the victims of abuse. The idea that it was the task of Christians to seek to transform the world by following the teaching of Jesus had largely faded into the past.

It was possibly partly in reaction to the decline of the traditional churches that there developed a number of new movements. One which became particularly important across both North and South America was the charismatic movement, which took off in the 1960s and is centred on a belief in the power of the Holy Spirit moving in the breasts of believers. It is important to many of its members but is not particularly relevant here, because its only contribution of any significance to Christian thinking is its emphasis on the importance of the Holy Spirit.

Another modern movement is fundamentalism, which in Christianity is primarily a matter of asserting with confidence the literal truth of everything in the Bible. It is an attitude which the ancient Greeks called *hubris* and which early Christians called pride and regarded as the most deadly of sins. When that attitude is seen as Christianity it does immense damage, in a way that the charismatic movement does not. There are, of course, fundamentalist Muslims, Atheists and Jews, and even fundamentalist Hindus and Buddhists. All of them would all impose their own views with force if they could. There is little to choose between them.

Far more important than either the charismatics or the fundamentalists was the evangelical movement. The word "evangelical" dates from the time of the Reformation when it referred to writers, both Catholic and Protestant, who consulted and quoted the Bible more often than had been customary for perhaps a thousand years. But in the twentieth century it came to describe a movement which not only emphasized the authority of the Bible but also stressed the importance of three other things: the idea that the death of Jesus on the cross paid the price for the sins of mankind, the need for personal conversion as the starting point for following him, and the obligation to seek to convert others.

It was not a new denomination, but rather an interdenominational movement whose members saw both theology and the way the church is organized as of secondary importance. They were concerned with mission, conversion and pastoral care rather than with theological issues, and the ultimate authority they recognised was the Bible. That could make evangelicals look suspiciously like fundamentalists, but whereas fundamentalists asserted the literal truth of what they saw as the Word of God, most evangelicals would try to understand the teaching of the Bible and put what they learnt into practice.

This understandably led to the idea that orthopraxis, or "correct practice", was more important than orthodoxy, or "correct doctrine", and to the view that behaving as Jesus had commanded was more important than getting one's ideas right. In itself that was entirely good, but it threw up two problems. One was that it had always been part of the Christian tradition that "good works" should be "the fruit of the spirit". That is, motives matter. To set up such groups as Sunday schools for children and young wives' clubs is entirely admirable if one's Christian faith has led one to believe that such things are desirable. To do so as a device for getting more people to come to church is not. It is a subtle distinction but an important one.

The other problem is that the emphasis on orthopraxis was too often accompanied not by toleration of varied theological opinions but by insistence on beliefs which had neither tradition nor rational thought to support them. A striking example of this is the widespread proclamation of what came to be known as the doctrine of atonement. For the first millennium and a half after Jesus the word "atonement" did not exist. It was coined in the early sixteenth century by William Tyndale, when he decided to translate the Latin word *reconciliatio*, or reconciliation, with a simple English word which he devised for that purpose: at-one-ment. He wanted to convey that the purpose of the crucifixion was that we should be at one with God and with our neighbours.

It is that idea, with "atonement" pronounced as it is written and with no memory of its original meaning, which was developed in America in the late nineteenth century into the idea that God was so angry about the sins of mankind that He decided to punish His own innocent Son, Jesus, by having him nailed to a cross to be tortured to death. It is a striking example of how badly things can go wrong when Christians assume, without thinking carefully, that they know the right answer to such an important issue as the reason for Jesus's crucifixion. They believe it in the manner of a prejudice and treat other explanations with contempt.

All Christians need an understanding of the significance of the cross, and it has long been possible to think of the crucifixion in a wide variety of ways: as a sacrifice, as triumph, as an example, and even as a logical necessity. In the middle of the nineteenth century Mrs C.F. Alexander, the wife of the Bishop of Derry, summarised four of them in the third verse of her hymn *There is a green hill far away*: "He died that we might be forgiven, he died to make us good, that we might go at last to heaven, saved by his precious blood". None of those explanations requires us to think of the Father being angry and punishing His Son while ignoring the Holy Spirit. They all express veneration for the sacrifice Jesus made when he went to the cross.

Dr J.S. Whale who was both a Congregational minister and a theologian, made that point forcibly when delivering a series of lectures on *Christian Doctrine* at Cambridge University in the autumn of 1940. He referred to the ideas of eighteen Christian thinkers, including Augustine of Hippo, Anselm, Aquinas, Luther and Calvin. All eighteen had over the centuries written about this crucial issue, and Whale ended his comments on their ideas by saying that "the crucial point is that none of these theological standpoints allows you to think of God as a cruel tyrant exacting his due from an innocent person on our behalf".

Perhaps in the twenty-first century the most helpful way to view the crucifixion is as both an example and a self-sacrifice. Jesus had annoyed the church leaders of his time by what he said and by what he did. He told them that, while meticulously obeying the Law, they had lost sight of the justice and love of God. He also turned over the traders' tables in the Temple, saying that his Father's house had been made a den of thieves. So the church leaders were determined to get rid of him. He could have avoided crucifixion. But he would neither change what he was teaching nor leave Jerusalem. He did not wish to die and said so explicitly. But if death was to be the consequence of standing by what he had been teaching, then he accepted it. It is an extraordinary example and an extraordinary act of self-sacrifice.

By going to his death as he did Jesus showed that it is possible to break the destructive cycle of recurring violence. Evil generates evil; violence generates violence; and the vicious, downward spiral of reciprocal violence is only broken when someone responds as Jesus did when he went to the cross with forgiveness and love. The way of life which he preached was explicitly based on forgiveness – on refusing to respond to violence with further violence, and he went to his death saying "Lord, forgive them, for they know not what they do". Atonement, or at-one-ment, should be the idea of mankind at one with God and with each other, following Jesus's example of forgiveness and reconciliation.

The early church was devoted to keeping the memory of Jesus alive. Two thousand years later the Christian churches still try to do so. But they are divided in any number of ways and over a wide range of issues. One cannot reasonably expect its members to abandon their various cherished beliefs. Pious Roman Catholics cannot be expected to give up their devotion to the papacy or to the Blessed Virgin Mary. Fervent evangelicals cannot be expected to give up their assurance in the authority of the Bible. Devoted members of the Orthodox churches cannot be expected to abandon their attachment to the doctrines and liturgy inherited from an ancient past. Much the same applies to the other Christian churches, whether Charismatics or Baptists or whatever else.

They can, however, reasonably be asked to be tolerant of, and even recognise as Christians, those many people who value the teaching of Jesus, try to live in accordance with it, and admire his self-sacrifice on the cross, but find it impossible to believe in the literal truth of traditional doctrines of the church such as the incarnation, the resurrection and the ascension, and do not understand what is meant by eternal or everlasting life.

One can also ask what, if anything, those who count themselves as Christians have in common. There is, perhaps, no right answer to this, for the variety of Christian belief is vast. But it may be worth offering a possibility. Above all they share an admiration for the teaching of Jesus, which includes an awareness of the Divine or, more specifically, the Being he referred to as his Heavenly Father. It also includes admiration for and acceptance of his commands about how to look at things and how to live, which for many people is summed up in the words of the twelfth verse of the seventh chapter of Matthew's gospel, often referred to as the Golden Rule: "In everything do to others as you would have them do to you". Finally they value, though in various different ways, his sacrifice on the cross.

These two things, his teaching and his self-sacrifice on the cross, are the essence of Christianity. All the conscientious and often very clever Christian thinking which has gone on and developed over two thousand years has led to disagreements about doctrine, authority, the creeds, the sacraments, morality, liturgy and prayer. But what Christian share is something which is the essence of Christianity and has been anonymously and beautifully summarized in a simple iambic pentameter: "the words of Jesus and his sacrifice".

Index

Dates in brackets refer either to events or else to a title, such as Emperor or Pope, which precedes the dates. All other dates refer to the duration of a person's life.

Orthodoxy, 69, 71, 76, 84, 123, 129, 174, 200
Orthopraxis, 129, 200
Ostrogoths, 76
Ottoman Turks, 122
Oxford, 6, 110, 115, 119, 167

Pagans, 49, 69, 73, 77, 81, 96
Paris, 104, 110, 111, 126, 140
Paris University, 111, 126, 140
Pascal II, Pope (1099–1118), 99
Patmos, 16
Patripassianism, 180
Paul the apostle, 31–45, 46, 47, 49, 52–54, 58, 91, 129, 131, 132, 134–136, 138, 151, 176, 179, 181, 184–186, 190, 191
Paul III. Pope (1534–49), 130
Pax Romana, 72, 92
Pelagianism, 85, 87, 89, 90
Pelagius, c. 354–c.420, 85, 89
Penance (one of seven sacraments), 127, 128, 131, 132, 191
Peter the apostle, 31–45, 123, 137, 196
Peter, First letter of, 42
Peter, Second letter of, 43
Petrarch, Francesco, 1304–1394, 118
Pharaoh, 184
Pharisees, 18, 20, 22, 23, 25, 26, 29, 31, 33, 36, 40

Philemon, 34, 53, 54
Philemon, Letter to, 34, 53, 54
Philosophy, 4, 9, 47, 55–58, 78, 80, 96, 98, 114–116, 128, 156, 160, 163, 164, 170
Philip the Apostle, 48
Philosphiae Naturalis Principia Mathematica, 161
Pietism, 150
Pilgrimage, 127, 131, 132
Pius II, Pope (1458–74), 123
Pius IX, Pope (1846–78), 172
Pius X, Pope (1903–14), 173
Pius XII, Pope (1939–58), 173
Plato c.470 BC–c.399 BC, 17, 56, 78, 113, 114, 116, 117, 156
plenitudo potestatis, 133
Pliny, 101
Pluralism, 127, 133
Poland, 4
Politics, 5, 10, 11, 55, 64, 88, 97, 123, 127, 128, 164, 171, 175, 182, 183
Polkinghorne, John, The Revd Professor, 1930–2021, 194
Pontius Pilate, Governor of Judea (26–36), 67
potentia absoluta, 116, 161
potentia ordinata, 116, 161
Predestination, 86, 89, 90, 141, 150, 153
Presbyterianism, 143, 146, 152
primus inter pares, 189

CHRISTIAN ALTERNATIVE
BOOKS

THE NEW OPEN SPACES

Throughout the two thousand years of Christian tradition
there have been, and still are, groups and individuals
that exist in the margins and upon the edge of faith. But
in Christianity's contrapuntal history it has often been
these outcasts and pioneers that have forged contemporary
orthodoxy out of former radicalism as belief evolves to engage
with and encompass the ever-changing social and scientific
realities. Real faith lies not in the comfortable certainties of
the Orthodox, but somewhere in a half-glimpsed hinterland
on the dirt track to Emmaus, where the Death of God meets
the Resurrection, where the supernatural Christ meets the
historical Jesus, and where the revolution liberates
both the oppressed and the oppressors.

Welcome to Christian Alternative... a space at the
edge where the light shines through.
If you have enjoyed this book, why not tell other readers
by posting a review on your preferred book site.

Christian Atheist
Belonging without Believing
Brian Mountford
Christian Atheists don't believe in God but miss him:
especially the transcendent beauty of his music,
language, ethics, and community.
Paperback: 978-1-84694-439-0 ebook: 978-1-84694-929-6

Compassion or Apocalypse?
A Comprehensible Guide to the Thoughts of
René Girard James Warren
How René Girard changes the way we think about
God and the Bible, and its relevance for our
apocalypse-threatened world.
Paperback: 978-1-78279-073-0 ebook: 978-1-78279-072-3

Diary Of A Gay Priest
The Tightrope Walker
Rev. Dr. Malcolm Johnson
Full of anecdotes and amusing stories, but the Church
is still a dangerous place for a gay priest.
Paperback: 978-1-78279-002-0 ebook: 978-1-78099-999-9

Readers of ebooks can buy or view any of these bestsellers by
clicking on the live link in the title. Most titles are published in
paperback and as an ebook. Paperbacks are available
in traditional bookshops. Both print and ebook
formats are available online.

Find more titles and sign up to our readers' newsletter at
www.collectiveinkbooks.com/christianity Follow us on
Facebook at https://www.facebook.com/ChristianAlternative